Missionary to Jamaica

Colin D. Standish

Hartland Publications

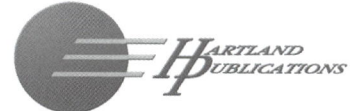

Copyright © 2007
Colin D. Standish

Cover design by
Greg Solie • AltamontGraphics.com

Text editing and layout by
Harvey Steck

Published by
Hartland Publications
PO Box 1, Rapidan, VA, 22733 USA
(540) 672-3566
Printed in USA

ISBN #0-923309-27-6

Contents

1. Jamaica Calling 5
2. Introduction to the United States 10
3. "Go Home, Porky!" 15
4. The Minister for Finance 19
5. "She's Devil Possessed" 23
6. Wonderful Integrity 27
7. Ordination to the Gospel Ministry 32
8. The Day the Mountain Shook 36
9. "I Don't Believe You" 39
10. Death Threats 44
11. New Challenges in Jamaica 51
12. Voodoo 56
13. I Wondered Whether I Would Die 59
14. Face to Face With a Rebel Leader in Anguilla 64
15. Death in the Hospital 67
16. "I Must Have My Quiver Full" 70
17. Blessed Experiences in Jamaica 75
18. More Jamaican Experiences 81
19. Demon Possession—Again 85
20. Sports in Jamaica 93
21. "Pastor! Pastor! Let Him Through!" 98
22. "I'll Pay You Back When I Sell the Crop" 104
23. "Be Careful, He's an Ignorant Man" 108
24. "That Will Be It For You" 112
25. "You'll Love It Until the Bloodbath Comes" 116

26. "I Plan to Do Nothing" 122
27. An Anachronism of the Past 128
28. The Great Deception. 131
29. "The Lord Gave, and the Lord Hath Taken Away" 137
30. Disagreements 142
31. Leaving. 146
32. Index 155
33. Hartland Publications Book List. 157
34. Meet the Authors 175

Jamaica Calling

1969

ABOUT September of 1969, one of the secretaries at the central office at Avondale College (Australia) came to inform me that I had an overseas phone call. I was very alarmed. Never, up to this time in my life, had I received a telephone call from overseas. Who could it be from? What would be the reason for the call?

My thoughts immediately turned to my twin brother Russell who was then a missionary doctor in the Penang Adventist Hospital in Malaysia. Had anything happened to him? Had he been injured or even worse? With great apprehension I approached the phone booth at the college. For some reason it took an agonizing six or seven minutes before the phone call eventually came through.

Without any introduction, the person phoning spoke with great enthusiasm concerning a desire to have me accept a call to be the academic dean of their college. What relief! After recovering from my anxiety, I waited expectantly. From where is this call coming? Who is this man who is talking with me? I knew he was not an Australian, but I could not identify the accent. I quickly dismissed the idea that he may have been from Asia because the voice did not sound like that of an Asian. I wondered whether he was calling from Africa. After ten minutes or more of dialogue, eventually I had to say, "You have not told me who you are, and from what country this call to service is coming." With apology he said, "This is your friend, Elder H.S. Walters, calling you from Jamaica."

What a shock! Never in my wildest dreams had I ever thought of being a worker in Jamaica. It seemed too far away. It seemed so remote. Yes, I would have understood a call to the South Pacific Islands, maybe even to Asia, even more remotely to Africa, but never had I dreamed of a call coming from the Caribbean.

It was true that my wife and I were interested in mission service. I was now serving my fifth year as chairman of the education department at Avondale College. During this time a call had been voted for me to become the first principal of Sonoma College in Papua New Guinea. However, the principal of Avondale College, Dr. Gordon McDowell had evaluated the situation and believed that I was far more needed at Avondale College than in this new college. I would have enthusiastically accepted that call, but having the belief that I should follow the decision of the brethren, I made no complaint when the principal of Avondale College refused to pass the call to me. However, this Jamaican call was an altogether different situation. The call did greatly interest me and also my wife Cheryl.

I knew little about the Caribbean. I knew that the Caribbean had a very strong cricket team which had toured Australia. I had heard of Calypso music, but I knew very little about Jamaica other than that the population was largely of African decent. I knew that many of the islands had been British colonies, which were now either becoming or had become independent nations. I knew the capital city was Kingston. However, that was about the extent of my knowledge. Yet, the call did excite us.

Very quickly, the principal of Avondale College heard about the call and came to do everything to convince me not to go. He even told me that if I served in a "black" college, I would never be invited to serve at an American college. I told him that if that was the attitude in America, I would not want to serve there. In any case, I had no desire to work in the United States. I told him that if a call came through to me I would accept it because I believed in accepting calls. Of course, I would be content to stay at Avondale College if the call was blocked. Dr. McDowell informed me that whereas he could block the call within the Australasian Division (now the South Pacific Division) there was a policy which forbade the blocking of calls which were passed through the General Conference from one division to another. No doubt this policy had been voted because many home fields were blocking calls to the mission field.

This call had come as a result of the fact that I had written to Pastor Robert Frame, an Australian, who was then an Associate Secretary of the General Conference, saying that if anything opened up for service overseas, I would be willing to respond. Clearly he had passed my name and particulars to the Inter-American Division or directly to the West Indies Union. In the course of time the call reached me and I wrote my acceptance, explaining that I could not commence until the end of January 1970.

Naturally, Cheryl and I desired to discover more about Jamaica. At this time, a Seventh-day Adventist physician, Dr. Gilbert McLaren, was practicing in the region close to Avondale College. He had served in Jamaica as president of the Andrews Memorial Hospital in Kingston and was the second Australian to serve in this capacity. Dr. Clifford Anderson had been the inaugural president of that hospital and was the twin brother of Pastor O.K. Anderson, a very dear friend of ours,.

When we spoke with the McLarens, they graciously invited us over to their home and told us they would tell us some of their experiences and also share with us some of the photos which they had brought from Jamaica. We accepted the invitation. We had a wonderful night there. However, during the course of the conversation, it became very obvious that the president of the West Indies Union was a man of great stature and powerful influence beyond what normally would have been expected. The McLarens shared with us some humorous stories of their own experience and they gave a generally positive report on their ministry in Jamaica.

Dr. Charles Hirsch, the then director of the Educational Department of the General Conference, visited Australia for year-end meetings in 1969. He visited Avondale College, and I took the opportunity to dialogue with him in the college room in which he was staying. I told him of my call to be academic dean of West Indies College (now North Caribbean University). Yes, he had visited there. He began walking around the room with his head bowed as he repeated several times, "So you'll be working with Tim Walters." "Tim" was the nickname of the West Indies Union president, Elder Hiram Sebastian Walters. He declined to comment further, but his comment and body language left an uneasy feeling about the kind of man the union president was.

Emotions were mixed as we neared the beginning of January, when we planned to leave for our entirely new experience. We were excited about this opportunity to explore a brand new world to us. However, there was the sorrow of leaving our friends and especially our family. It was particularly difficult for Cheryl, as she is an only child, and it was very hard for her parents to know that their one and only daughter would be 10,000 miles away in a strange country which they did not know. I assured them that the Lord would be with us and protect us.

We did not go directly to Jamaica. We decided we would do a little exploring. Up until this point of our lives, the only other place we had traveled to was New Zealand. Therefore, we were hardly international travelers. Our flight was to take us to Fiji, Honolulu, and Los Angeles from where we had arranged to purchase a $99 Greyhound ticket each, which was good for 30 days to travel through the United States from the Los Angeles area to Miami, from where we would fly to Jamaica. All too soon, January 6 arrived. It certainly was a sad and emotional farewell, especially for Cheryl and her parents.

The first leg of our journey was on an Air India flight to Nadi (pronounced Nandi), the International Airport in Fiji, on a Boeing 707. This flight had come from India, to Perth, to Sydney, and would terminate in Nadi, Fiji. Air India traveled frequently to Fiji because more than half the population of Fiji is now Indian.

Shortly after the commencement of the flight, the hostess walked through the cabin, asking for a show of hands of all those who were vegetarian. This was obviously a regular duty of the hostess, because many Indians are vegetarian. Of course, we raised our hands, and in quite a surprised voice, the hostess said, "Are you serious?" We assured her that we were serious. She told us it was more than two years since she had had any white person order a vegetarian meal. How things have changed in nearly four decades!

We had arranged to stay a number of days in Fiji. Our arrival coincided with the "Bose," the Fijian name for their camp meeting. Even though it was not arranged in advance, nevertheless, they rearranged the schedule so

I could make two presentations at the camp meeting. It was a very pleasant and warm environment. We greatly enjoyed being in the tropics for the first time in our lives, with all its fruits and its attractive scenery.

The next leg of our journey was to Honolulu. Of course we had heard much about Honolulu and what a wonderful place it was. However, it was altogether new to us. We rented a car for the day to tour around the regions of the island of Oahu. This was my first experience of driving on the right side of the road. I could not imagine how difficult it was going to be to readjust my thinking. You can be assured that I drove very slowly and very carefully and stopped at every turn I had, to make sure which direction to follow. We were again impressed with the splendor of the scenery as we drove around much of the island. We visited the Mormon Center, which also was quite interesting to us.

There was one aspect of our arrival in Hawaii which was very enlightening. When we arrived, we could not understand why the women were dressing in such an old fashioned way. At this time, very few women on the streets in America were wearing pants. We had left Australia, where at this time, the microskirts, less than twelve inches from the waist, were commonly worn by the younger ladies and teenagers especially, and most of the more "modest" were wearing miniskirts. Of course, we applauded such obvious modest dress in Hawaii; yet somehow our eyes had adapted to shorter dresses. We found that most of the women in Honolulu were wearing dresses well below the knee. It was a wake up call to us to realize that our eyes had unwittingly become adapted to such immodesty in dress that when we saw a majority of women dressed modestly, we thought they looked old fashioned, even dowdy. How careful we must always be to keep in mind the true principles of Heaven!

There was another issue which quite surprised us. For the first time in our experience, we found that when we ordered a cool drink, a liberal quantity of ice was placed in the drink. We had never experienced this in Australia. Our first thoughts were that the people were robbing us. We soon became used to the differences in culture and we realized just how unilateral our experience up to that time had been.

We left Honolulu on a United stretch DC 8 to Los Angeles—our first visit to the mainland of the United States.

Introduction to the United States

OF course, we had heard much about the United States before our first visit. Yet, we certainly were not prepared for our introduction to this country.

We had Australian friends in Loma Linda who met us at Los Angeles Airport. We made our way to Loma Linda for the weekend with these friends. Our first Sabbath in the United States was at the Loma Linda University Church. It left us somewhat shaken by the presentation which was made in the Sabbath School class to which we were taken. We found out that the man was a popular teacher and presenter, and many attended his class, but we sensed in his Sabbath School class that he was espousing many alien views, though he was a professor at Loma Linda University. This was a great disappointment to us and confirmed what we had heard by many rumors in Australia about the liberal, worldly approaches of Seventh-day Adventists in the United States, especially California. It would be only years later that we would find that some of the finest Seventh-day Adventists whom one could meet anywhere in the world also live in the southern part of California.

It was our journey across the country which gave us the initial negative impression of the United States. We were not ready for our first few days in this country. We almost wondered whether we would reach Miami alive.

We had boarded the Greyhound Bus at San Bernardino, which took us to the large Greyhound Terminal in Los Angeles. By the time we arrived, it was close to midnight. Not long after we arrived, quite a scene developed. A man, heavily under the influence of alcohol, had apparently locked some personal effects in one of the lockers at the bus station. He had lost his key. He demanded that the staff open his locker, but of course he did not have the number of the locker, and being such a large station, it was virtually impossible to help him. He became quite verbally aggressive at this point in time and the security officer took charge of the situation. We were shocked when the drunk was shoved against a concrete pillar and the back of his head cracked against the concrete. We were shaken by such undue force. The security officer being sober could have easily handled him without going to that degree of force.

We traveled overnight to Sacramento. In Sacramento a man took the seat beside me. He looked very strange indeed. However, I tried to engage him in conversation, and asked him whether he lived in Sacramento. No, he lived in Montana. I asked whether he had been visiting friends in the Sacramento area. No, he'd been on trial. Trying to continue the conversation I asked, "Oh, what was the charge against you." With a sardonic laugh he said, "Murder." As I tried to hold my composure, I said to him, "Well, obviously you were found not guilty." Still showing the same sardonic attitude he said, "They can't find you guilty if they don't find a body, can they?" I do not have to tell you I felt a rather uncomfortable feeling sitting with him for many hours. I really began to wonder what kind of people lived in the United States.

We were approaching the middle of January as our bus headed across the United States on Highway 80, climbing up and over the Sierra Nevadas at night. It was intensely cold outside; however, the bus was comfortable. Eventually, we reached Utah. While crossing the barren region of Utah, the bus stopped unexpectedly in a desolate area. A police car was waiting, and the policemen quickly boarded the bus and escorted two struggling men off the bus into the bitter cold. As the bus sped off, the last view we had of the men was with their hands over the top of the police car as the officers frisked them. We learned that these men had been drinking alcohol against the bus company rules, and the driver had radioed to the police. However, you can understand with three such incidences in a short space of time, we certainly were seeing a side of a country so different from what we had been used to in Australia.

For the rest of our journey, we did not have any other incidents like these, even though most of the bus stations in the large cities were not in the most favorable parts of those cities. We eventually reached Cleveland, Ohio where we stayed overnight in the home of Dr. and Mrs. Barton Rippon. They were Seventh-day Adventists, and I had been at Sydney University with Dr. Barton. He was now undertaking post-doctoral work in Cleveland. Unbeknown to us was the fact that in the weekend newspaper, Sister Rippon had advertised baby care at her home—a way to make a little extra money for her family. We were shocked the next morning when a woman, with her two week old baby knocked at the door. She had no idea who the Rippons were, whether they were trustworthy people or not. She was going back to work that morning, she read the ad, and she arrived to leave her baby in their custody. We were amazed at what we believed was the total irresponsibility of this mother. Of course, a lot has happened in society since that incident more than 35 years ago. Although that kind of thinking probably would not shock the reader at this time, it certainly shocked us at that time.

We then moved on to State College in Pennsylvania where Pennsylvania State University is located. There we were to meet up with a Sydney University colleague, Dr. Brian Crabbe, who was undertaking post-doctorate work at the University. We arrived at the tiny bus station in zero-degree weather. Keep in mind we did not grow up in this kind of winter. Unfortunately our friend missed the time of our arrival, and we wondered whether we would freeze to death, for the bus shelter was not heated. However, we survived, and he arrived about an hour later. We could not have been happier to meet our friend.

From there it was on to New York and down to Washington where we stayed with Elder and Mrs. Ernest Steed. Elder Steed was then the director of the Temperance Department of the General Conference. He being an Australian, we had known him in earlier years. We stayed a couple of days in Washington and there we had the opportunity to meet members of the Educational Department of the General Conference. I especially met with Dr. Walter Brown who had been the educational director of the Inter-American Division before being elected to the General Conference. He was very happy to talk with me concerning the issue of my appointment to West Indies College. He made it very plain that it was important for me to work very closely with the union president, Elder H.S. Walters. Dr. Brown's comment added to a building apprehensiveness concerning the union president under whom I would serve. What seemed strange to me was that he said very little concerning Elder Kenneth Vaz, the president of the college. Of course I believed that it was my first responsibility to work closely with the president of the college. Later I think I understood why he had given me that counsel.

We had no further stops until we reached Miami, and there we caught an Air Jamaica flight, flew over Cuba, and landed at Sangster International Airport (Montego Bay, Jamaica) before continuing on to the Norman Washington Manly International Airport, just outside Kingston, in the Port Royal area of Jamaica. After clearing immigration and customs, we were happy to see the sign with our names on it. Pastor Vaz was there to meet and greet us. We then had the opportunity to get to know each other a little on the two-hour journey back to the center of Jamaica, to the Parish of Manchester, the city of Manderville, near where West Indies College is located.

I must admit that we were not a little uneasy during the drive to the college. We had not been in a country before where animals, birds, cattle, goats and chickens meandered across the road. It seemed to us that almost certainly we would have a collision with one or more of these. Yet, that did not happen. Somehow it would seem that at the last moment the bird or animal would veer just out of harm's way, or the driver would veer slightly to miss the offending animal. Of course, we soon learned the ways of Jamaican driving. It was far more important for us to learn the unwritten rules than the written rules. One always expects the written rules to be somewhat similar from one country to another. At least we were back in a country in which drivers drove on the left side of the road as we did in Australia.

It took us a little while to get used to the unwritten rules, however. Very early in our stay there, we had a very close call. The rules were quite plain—that is, the legal rule: the first vehicle which reaches a narrow, one-lane bridge has the right of way. Taking this for granted, I came onto a bridge, and a truck decided to keep powering ahead onto this bridge, even though we were already on it. I squeezed over as far as I possibly could. I believed there was every chance that we would be hit; yet somehow, at the last moment, we avoided that head-on collision. I believe the angels had to do a little contracting of the vehicles or widening of the bridge. I soon learned that "might was right." Never again did I drive onto a one-way bridge if any big vehicle was anywhere near the bridge. I would wait for that vehicle to cross.

We were temporarily placed in a very comfortable home next to the college president until another one was to open up several months later. We found the surroundings very attractive and the accommodations of good quality, although Cheryl was not used to the spiders which frequented our dwelling. In the end, she learned to live rather uncomfortably with them.

We had hardly arrived at our new home when I spotted a large man with a broad smile coming toward me. Intuitively I guessed it was Elder H.S. Walters, the union president. He looked younger than his 48 years. Of course he was very friendly and gave us a very warm welcome. He addressed my wife, Cheryl, as "mistress," a term she soon became used to, especially from Elder Walters.

We became good friends with the college president's dog Khrushchev. Khrushchev was a German Shepard, called after a leader of the Soviet Union, Nikita Khrushchev. He had a very discriminative approach to people. He was very friendly to well dressed men and to all the ladies. However, any man of the poorer people, or any man who was dressed in work clothes, he would attack very viciously. He certainly was a good guard dog, and of course, in Jamaica, such dogs are highly prized.

Now we were ready to begin our new experience in a new country, in a new culture. What a fascinating set of experiences stretched before us!

"Go Home, Porky!"

1970

AS you can imagine, when my wife and I arrived in Jamaica we were in a world totally different from the world in which we had been born and reared. In 1970 Australia was still overwhelmingly Caucasian, with the strong majority of citizens being of British-Irish descent. That is still true today. However, the percentages have changed significantly. In Jamaica we were in a nation which is dominantly of African background. We soon found, however, that most of the people were very friendly and welcomed us with open arms. However, from time to time as we traveled in the countryside of Jamaica, it was very common for children to call out, "Whitey" or "Porky." This was a mildly derogative term for white people because pork is of a light pink color.

Soon we had been five weeks at West Indies College. We were adjusting to the different ways of doing things and a different way of thinking as is always necessary when one is in a culture different from that of his own. On Saturday night we attended a special social program. After the program, the director of the cafeteria—Mrs. Cheeseman—came to talk with me, as the president, Elder Vaz, was not present at the function. She pointed out that the young ladies working in the cafeteria, in their haste to get to the program, had not cleaned up the cafeteria before they had repaired to the program. The cafeteria had been left in a terrible mess with utensils and dishes not washed and the stoves not cleaned, the floors not swept.

Mr. And Mrs. Cheeseman had been working for a number of years at West Indies College by this time. The Cheesemans were English by birth, but toward middle life they had migrated to Canada and it was from Canada that they accepted the call to West Indies College, Sister Cheeseman to be the cafeteria director, Brother Cheeseman to head the wood products industry. Both were dedicated Christians; both were capable in the areas in which they were serving. We were to become very good friends of the Cheesemans although they were to return to Canada less than six months after we arrived. Even to this day, occasionally I am in contact with Mrs. Cheeseman, Brother Cheeseman having passed away from Parkinson's disease some years ago. [Note: As we go to press, I have received word that Sister Cheeseman passed away September 2006.]

Being very new at West Indies College, I asked her what would normally be done in such a circumstance. She believed that the young ladies responsible for leaving the cafeteria in a mess should be required to clean it up before they went to sleep. I decided to talk with one of the Jamaican staff members to make sure I was making a decision which was acceptable in the new society in which I was living. This staff member said very adamantly, "The girls are probably in bed now but they need to be gotten out of bed and do the work they did not do before the social program." Thus I asked the dean of women and she agreed that that was the right thing to do, and the girls were required to get out of bed, get dressed again and come to the cafeteria to clean it up so that it would be ready for the morning breakfast.

This was done, and I thought nothing more about it—that is, until about midmorning on Sunday when my wife and I returned to the campus. We were absolutely taken aback. There was an angry demonstration on the campus. The looks of many young people were that of hostility. As my wife and I walked up the campus, a number of the students took up stones and rolled them at us, not to hurt us but to show their objection to us. There were signs up, "Go home, Porky." This was no doubt a reaction to the disciplinary decision I had made the night before. Certainly it was exacerbated by the fact that the two families involved—the Cheesemans and the Standishes—were white people.

This was a shocking experience for us. We had never expected it. We had never seen students react with such hostility in our educational ministry before, and, to say the least, it was a perplexing and difficult situation. We wondered whether we had done the right thing to come to Jamaica. We even contemplated that it might be safer for us to return to Australia. However, this we did not do because we realized that God had called us to Jamaica, and we were confident in His protection and in the fact that we had done what we believed to be the right thing the night before. However, it was a most unpleasant experience. We wondered how we could serve effectively if we had such hostility from the students. We were to find generally speaking, however, that though there were those students who were volatile among the student body, not all students felt the same way. Also, we learned that often while the emotions would flare, very frequently they would subside just as quickly.

When the union president learned what had happened, he called a meeting of all the student body the next day. Only as Elder H.S. Walters could do, he spoke passionately to the students, expressing his disgust with what had transpired the day before. He exhorted the students to behave far more responsibly, expressed zero toleration for this kind of conduct, and he would make sure that if this happened again, those students responsible would be expelled from the college. There was no appeal to the student body; it was purely a demand.

The president of the United Student Movement—the student body organization—also strongly condemned the actions of the day before, telling the students that the United Student Movement would not support them in such actions and that the behavior of those involved was not the way to treat those who had come to serve at West Indies College and to be a blessing to the educational program there. That was the end of the incident. A number of the students apologized to us. Never again were we to have such a hostile reaction to us. God was good, and we greatly appreciated His guidance and leading in that difficult situation.

What a difference was our later departure from West Indies College! Indeed, so many of the students came to express their sadness that we were leaving. This was especially made evident to us as we returned from a trip to Kingston not long before we left Jamaica. When we arrived back, five students were in our driveway. When I alighted from our car, in chorus the young people said, "Welcome home, Mr. President." I laughed and said, "You have left out a little two-word prefix." I was referring to the prefix "ex." I was greatly moved by the response of these students. They said, "No, you will always be our president." Such was the love and dedication of these students to my wife and me. We found exactly the same response from the staff. Many of them wanted to form a delegation to go to the Union office to protest the circumstances in which we were leaving. They knew it was because of my opposition to the reelection, by dishonest manipulation, of the union president. But I urged them not to do so. I told them that if they really appreciated my leadership at the college they would honor my request that they be silent regarding the fact that I was leaving. Overall our experience at West Indies College was a most profitable experience. I have often said that we received ten years experience in three plus years. That was hardly an exaggeration, for I learned so much in this my first responsibility as the leader of an educational institution.

The Minister for Finance

1970

DURING the latter part of 1970, arrangements were made for a number of West Indies College staff to visit Gordon House, the Parliament of Jamaica. I had not visited previously, so I was interested to observe a little of the parliamentary proceedings. Mrs. Lucille Walters knew quite a number of the parliamentarians who had either been or were now Seventh-day Adventists or who had studied at West Indies College. She made the arrangements for our visit. She was the registrar of the college and the wife of the West Indies union president, Hiram Sebastian (Tim) Walters.

On what proved to be a very fascinating day, we met a number of the members of parliament, such as Dr. Neville Gallimore, with whom my wife and I were developing a friendship. He was the member for Southeastern St. Anne, the southeastern section of the Parish of St. Anne, a north-central parish in Jamaica. For the first time I met Mr. Hill, a graduate of West Indies College who was no longer a practicing Seventh-day Adventist. He was a huge man. At that time he was the Minister for Housing in the Jamaican government. However, the most fascinating man whom we met was Mr. Edward Seaga. He was the Minister for Finance in the Jamaica Labor Party government and was destined later to become the prime minister of Jamaica.

There were many reasons for me to be interested in this man. Firstly, he was an ethnic Syrian. I found it quite interesting that a man who held the second most important office in the government was not of African descent, but from Syrian descent, and that he was, not too long after this visit, to become the leader of the Jamaica Labor Party. It was also astounding to realize that the leader of the opposition, People's National Party, Michael Manley, was a very light-skinned black. His father, Norman Washington Manley, had been declared to be one of the five great national heroes of Jamaica. He had never achieved the office of Prime Minister of Jamaica as his son did, though as leader of the opposition party he had done much to help in the development of independence for the nation of Jamaica.

Norman Washington Manley was also a light-skinned black who had married an English wife, so you can understand why his son Michael was very light skinned. Here was a nation dominated by people of African heritage, yet at this time the leaders of the two major parties were on the one hand white and the other one almost white. But both were strongly supported by their parties.

It was sad, however, to meet Mr. Seaga, a man who once had been a Seventh-day Adventist. I already knew his sister because she lived in Mandeville where West Indies College is located. The sister conducted a travel agency which I visited frequently to acquire bookings for various travels. She, too, sadly had left the Seventh-day Adventist Church and was now a smoker. To add to the sadness of it, she had attended Southern Missionary College (now Southern Adventist University) as a young woman. When she had initially applied at Southern Missionary College, she was turned down because they naturally assumed that she was black, and in those days black students were not accepted at that college. I believe this had a negative impact upon her as a Christian. At least as she related it to me she was quite negative to the situation at Southern Missionary College of that era.

While at Southern Missionary College she had had a romantic interlude with a man who is a well-known member of the Adventist-Laymen's Services and Industries (ASI) in the United States. Indeed, while I was president of West Indies College, he visited Jamaica not to visit this woman, for he had no idea where she was, but since she had mentioned his name to me, when he came to the college I told him where this lady was located. He was interested to meet her again after many years—probably at least 20 years since they were in college together.

Now, back to the visit to Gordon House—the Parliament of Jamaica. While we were talking with Mr. Seaga at Gordon House, he asked, "Would you like to come for a walking tour through my constituency?" Now, it so happened that he was the member for West Kingston, notorious for being the center of crime in Jamaica and the most dangerous and violent part of all Jamaica, but we accepted his offer. He had an astounding record. Prior to becoming the member for West Kingston, every member had lasted only one term because these people were so dissatisfied with the performance of their members. However that was not the case with Seaga. He had been reelected a number of times to five-year terms of office.

As we walked through his constituency, he walked as if he was a demigod. Wherever he walked, people came, almost falling at his feet. Two young women came in great adoration and walked with him holding on, one on one arm and the other on the other arm. It was not that he was looking for a romantic attachment. He had a very beautiful wife. She had been Miss Jamaica before he married her. He showed us the apartment buildings he had had built for the people. He told us that they had been living under tin and cardboard before he built these apartment buildings. Even though the apartment buildings were not grand by normal western standards, yet they represented a remarkable advance from the terrible living conditions which many of the people in West Kingston had endured prior to his election as the member for West Kingston.

I noticed as we walked, he was using chalk to mark crosses here and there. I asked him for what purpose he was doing this. He responded, "I always do this when I am walking through the constituency. I built this education and sports center" (one of the features which he proudly showed to us). "If I see any dirt marks I put a cross and the people know that they have to clean that before I return. If I come back and see the cross still there I have to hold them accountable." He certainly was a remarkable presence. It would be hard to find more dedicated people than the people of West Kingston to their elected member of Parliament.

Yet there was another side to this man. There was much talk that he had used his role as Minister for Finance to apply huge amounts of the national budget into raising the standard of living in his constituency.

That was most likely correct because of the great improvements he had made in this very needy part of the city of Kingston. There are other much more attractive, modern areas of Kingston, but one could hardly begrudge these people the improvement which Mr. Seaga had made.

Jamaica is a large producer of bauxite which is transported to the United States of America and Canada for refinement into aluminum. There were both American and Canadian companies operating in the country. The manager of one of the Canadian companies told me that Mr. Seaga sent many of his ruffians from West Kingston with a note demanding that he employ them. He said he had no alternative but to do so, and that meant many of the much better class of men in the center part of Jamaica could not be employed because of these demands from Mr. Seaga. There was also the report that before the previous election, Mr. Seaga had smuggled many guns into Jamaica from Cuba in what at first appeared to be large cans of powered milk, and then he had distributed them to some of his constituents. If true it was indeed an extraordinarily irresponsible act.

While we were walking, I asked him whether he still had any thought about his upbringing in the Seventh-day Adventist Church. "Oh, yes," he said, "I remember it very well" and then he began to sing little parts of some hymns which he learned when a youth. It was clear, however, that he had put a political career—maybe a very questionable career—before his own salvation.

Numbers of times my wife and I visited the Andrews Memorial Church which was located in the grounds of the Andrews Memorial Hospital (a Seventh-day Adventist institution). Mr. Seaga's dear mother was a faithful member of that church. My heart went out to her. Here were two children, both brought up in the Seventh-day Adventist faith but both having chosen the world.

> For what shall it profit a man, if he shall gain the whole world, and lose his own soul? Or what shall a man give in exchange for his soul? Mark 8:36–37

"She's Devil Possessed"

1970

I HAD just recently assumed the Presidency of West Indies College. It was during the summer recess of 1970 when a young lady knocked on my office door and asked whether she could talk with me. I knew her a little. She was an eighteen-year-old young lady by the name of Vivienne. She had graduated a few weeks before from West Indies high school and was planning to attend college in the autumn. She worked at the college over the summer to help build up fees, having been accepted as a freshman to commence college September of that year.

After we prayed she told me that she was afraid. Often she heard voices speaking to her, telling her to do things which were dangerous, including to jump out the second story window of the young ladies' dormitory. She said that often the voices were telling her to stand by the mandarin tree. There was one small mandarin tree on the campus. It was between the administrative buildings and the young men's dormitory. It was close to a steep fall of at least 200 or 300 feet. She said that when she was there, she was told often to jump over this steep cliff. It was obvious that she was being harassed, at the least, by satanic agencies. Yet God and His angels were protecting her, holding her back from doing what the devil was urging for her self-destruction.

I talked with her about the power of Christ, about her prayer life and her devotional life in studying the things of God. Suddenly, however, as I was speaking I looked at her again and her eyes were glazed; she stood up like a robot, walked out of my office, and down the hallway. It took me a little time to realize what was taking place. I followed and noticed that she was walking toward the young ladies' dormitory. I quickly returned to my office, alerted the dean of women and said, "Something is wrong with Vivienne. Please be there to meet her when she comes into the dormitory." Before she came into my office she had been practicing the organ at the college and had been playing from the score of the Messiah. She had left that music on the seat in my office. I told the dean of women, "If you have any problems, please alert me."

About ten minutes later the dean of women called me in great distress. She said, "Vivienne is tearing up everything religious in her room. Please come and help me." I immediately responded to this call for help. On the way I met the dean of men, Elder Oswald Rugless, and then Elder Hilbert Nembhard, chairman of the religion department. I said, "Brethren, come with me. We have a problem with one of the students." They hastened with me to the young ladies' dormitory, up the stairs to the second floor to Vivienne's room, and there we saw magazines, even Bibles and hymnbooks torn to pieces. Yet anything secular or nonreligious, whether it be reading material or clothes, she was neatly placing in her suitcase. What indicated that it was supernatural was the fact that her eyes were turned up to the ceiling and yet she made no mistakes. Always if the object was religious she was tearing it to pieces; if it was nonreligious, she was folding it and placing it carefully in a suitcase. This had to be the miraculous hands of a devil.

I tried to talk with her, but there was absolutely no response. She was acting as if she did not hear. I asked the dean of women, "Please, go before her and find anything that is religious and take it out of harm's way." We wondered what to do. I suggested we call the Union office just half a mile away where her older sister worked as a secretary. When I explained the situation to the sister, she assured me she had never seen anything like this behavior from Vivienne. I asked her to come to Vivienne's room to see whether she could help us in any way.

While I was downstairs telephoning the sister, suddenly Vivienne had made a break for the door and raced away. The elders were not sure whether she had come downstairs or gone along the corridor upstairs, for there was a ground level exit for the second floor at the other end of the dormitory. I assured them she had not come downstairs, so we knew she was making a dash to somewhere, maybe onto the road where she could be a danger to herself. I quickly placed the dean of women and the other two brethren in a car, and we drove along the campus. There she was, standing by the mandarin tree which she had mentioned to me just a short while before.

I slowly approached her and began to talk with her, but once again there was absolutely no response. It was as if I was not there. At that point I began to pray for I knew the only help we could rely upon was help from the Lord Jesus Christ. When the prayer was completed I noticed that she seemed to be coming out from the haze of her mind, and increasingly she was understanding what I was saying and paying attention to my words. Eventually I was able to ask her, "Vivienne, how did you get here?" She answered, "I don't know." "From where did you come to be here?" After some hesitation she said, "I think I came from your office." It was obvious she had no recollection of what she had done after she had left my office and the chaos she had created in her dormitory room. I said, "Vivienne, let us go back to your dormitory room." We placed her in the car and took her back without giving her any information concerning the carnage she had wrought in the room.

When we reached the room, she saw the mess and chaos in the room. With great horror she recoiled and turned to me with a pitiful voice asking, "Did I do all that?" I said, "Yes, Vivienne, you did that. Let us sit on the bed and talk about it." There the four of us began to discuss the situation with her. Soon after we began to dialogue, her sister arrived very distressed about the situation. As I began to explain to Vivienne that she had no other option but to surrender everything to the Lord, suddenly, without warning, again she made a wild dash to the door. But I grabbed her. Though the young lady was slender but tall, and even though I was still only in my 30s, I found it almost impossible to hold her. I called for the other two men, "Please help me." Between the three of us we were able to wrestle her back and throw her body across the bed. I pinned her on one shoulder and the dean of men on the other and I asked the dean of women to hold her legs down to keep her modest. Then I asked Elder Nembhard, "Elder, please pray." He prayed the most beautiful prayer asking God to give this young lady freedom from the devils who were possessing her.

Suddenly the violent struggle stopped. Acquiescence came over her but huge beads of perspiration were on her brow and her breathing was extremely labored. Shortly afterwards she came out of the trance. Before the struggle ceased, her body convulsed violently from the top of her body down to her feet as if the devils were leaving her from the top of her head, through her body, down her legs and through her toes. It was then that we were able to speak with her earnestly.

We explained the mighty power of prayer and how God had so wonderfully relieved her of this spirit possession through the intervention of Elder Nembhard's prayer and above all the divine mediation of our Lord Jesus Christ. I explained to Vivienne that whatever had led her into this spiritism it was not necessary for her to tell us, but she must break every tie with whatever had led to that situation. I believe she did just that.

For the next several years as a student at West Indies College she was an exemplary student, doing well academically, with not the slightest recurrence of that which had taken place that summer day in 1970. There is power, great power, mighty power, divine power, in the name of our Lord Jesus Christ.

Wonderful Integrity

1971

AS I have indicated before, my wife and I were the only white faculty members for most of the time we were on the staff at West Indies College. Most faculty were of African descendent but a number of them had at least some east Indian heritage. I would be remiss in writing this book without acknowledging some of the fine Christians with whom we served. Most of the time I was president, Dr. Herman Douce was the academic dean. Dr. Douce was a man of fine spiritual leadership and one who was more than a colleague; he was a friend. I admired his calm and Christlike disposition and his ability to offer me counsel from time to time which proved to be valuable to me.

I was also privileged to have two colleagues working with me in the business leadership. Elder Aston Davis was business manager and Brother Aston Barnes was the treasurer. Brother Barnes was later to become the treasurer of the West Indies Union. You can understand that in a relatively poor country like Jamaica the financial leadership played a very critical role. There was never enough money for the operation of the college. The students' fees at the time for a year of room, board and tuition was only the equivalent of about 600 United States dollars. Even with the most careful economy, that was not sufficient for the operation of the college. There were some subsidies from the Union, but too often the college was strapped for funds. It was not an easy assignment. However, with little complaint these men labored carefully to hold a tight reign upon the finances. They were leaders of integrity. Never did I question the possibility of any dishonesty by either one of them. Sometimes in countries where the economy is weak, there are temptations to appropriate funds from God's work into the pockets of those who have access to them, but I had no reason to question their integrity in the years I was working with these men. Both men had capable wives who also made big contributions in the work of the institution. Sister Zenobia Davis was chairperson of the music department, an excellent pianist and choir director. Sister Linnie Barnes was an excellent teacher in the academy.

Two other men who made an indelible impact upon me were Elder Hilbert Nembhard, chairman of the religion department and Elder Oswald Rugless, the dean of men. It would be rare to work with two finer Christians than these men. Elder Rugless had been dean of men for fifteen years with a short interlude between two terms of service. Even today, when I think of deans with whom I have worked—and some of them did very good work—somehow Elder Rugless, to me, was *the* dean, the man of unwavering principle and of courage no matter what the situation was. He had a way of retaining the respect of the young men even when he was speaking strongly to them about some infraction of the rules. Elder Rugless talked to me about retiring from that position because it was a constant strain, but I could not imagine having another one to replace a man of his stature and caliber. He eventually agreed to carry on. I have often wondered whether I was responsible for his premature death because, less than two years after I left, this grand man of God was taken in death while still in his 50s.

Pastor Hilbert Nembhard was a man who sincerely believed the Seventh-day Adventist faith. He had a steadfast trust but an appropriate sense of humor. He was faithful to the pillars of the Seventh-day Adventist faith, and I knew that with him the ministerial students were in good hands. He was a very kindly man and very solicitous of the young men with whom he had been entrusted to train for the next generation of gospel ministers.

Elder Nembhard and Elder Rugless both had excellent wives. Sister Millicent Nembhard was a stalwart in the academy and Sister Admah Rugless was the leader of the college secretarial department. One of the most vivid memories I have of these two elders were the occasions when they were presiding at the divine service Sabbath morning. As was the custom at the college church, the platform party walked from the back of the chapel down the center aisle and up onto the platform. How to explain the thrill it was to see these two men with such contrasting bearing walking to that platform. Both had a godly dignity about them! Elder Rugless, with his straight back, was a man who walked with great grace. Elder Nembhard had the professorial, slightly bent over image as he walked up. Both equally reflected the solemnity of the responsibility of presiding at the divine service. It was a great privilege years later when Elder Nembhard, then pastoring in the Southern California Conference, dedicated our son Nigel to the Lord. In 2005 he passed to his rest well over 80 years old.

I should not ignore my predecessor, Elder Kenneth Vaz. Elder Vaz had been president for six years at a time when the previous five presidents served no more than one and a half years, so turbulent were those years. Elder Vaz had brought a steady solidarity to the direction of the college, and it was a great honor to follow him as president. Even when he left to do evangelism and pastoral work and later departmental work at the Union, his wife remained as a very effective and intelligent librarian at the college. They were a couple to be admired and were among a few leaders who were vegetarians. Sister Vaz passed away before the writing of this book.

Even though you cannot picture any of these people as you read this book, unless the reader be an older West Indian, nevertheless, I hope you can capture the great regard and respect I held for these colleagues with whom I worked.

Maybe the colleague with whom I served who most epitomized the spirit of West Indies College was Sister Lucille Walters. She was the wife of the union president. Born in New York City to West Indian parents, she never did, to the best of my knowledge, have any official Jamaican status. She was so respected and so well known in the nation that no one ever worried that she failed to carry a Jamaican passport or work permit in and out of the country. If she was challenged by a young new immigration officer she would simply say, "I'm more Jamaican than you are." Thus if anyone were to symbolize West Indies College during my presidency, it was Sister Walters. She was not only registrar, she was an outstanding history teacher. She seemed to know every student who had ever passed through that college. We could always tell when a graduate was returning to the college, for Sister Walters' excitement would reverberate down the corridors of the office block. Of course, she would bring the individual or individuals to introduce them to me. Many a needy student would be accommodated in her home to help them in their training for the work of the Lord. Lucille Walters was Mrs. West Indies College, a unique one of a kind. She passed away a good many years ago in her seventies.

There were other fine college personnel. There was the dean of women, Sister Daisy White, who, like Elder Rugless, carried a heavy burden in the care of the large number of young ladies she "mothered." She was truly a fine dean of women. Who of that generation of students and staff at West Indies College would ever forget Sister Lourine Chisholm, leader of the English division? She was more British than the British themselves. She spoke with great precision and eloquence. She was a wonderful reader of either poetry or prose. Sometimes the students felt she was too strict. Some of the students were disturbed because she strongly believed that no student should speak patois—the local common language of Jamaica—on the campus, but Miss Chisholm was not someone with whom to argue, and the students greatly respected her. She knew how to teach the Queen's English to those students. There is no question in my mind that she laid a wonderful foundation for many of the young men who were to become powerful preachers—quite a few of whom have been successful pastors and leaders in various parts of the world.

Another impressive individual was Sister Edna Parchment. She came from a very well known Seventh-day Adventist family in Jamaica and was the chairperson of the business department. Under her leadership the business department flourished, and her graduates were in great demand both denominationally and in the community of Jamaica at large. Always it was believed that they were among the best trained in Jamaica. She too has passed to her rest along with Sister Chisholm.

What a lovable woman was Sister Del Brodie (Aunt Del to many)! She and her sister Glad (Aunt Glad) served in the work in Jamaica for many years. Aunt Glad was the matron of the Andrews Memorial Hospital in Kingston while we served in Jamaica. Sister Brodie was a friend to everybody and was frequently carrying out acts of kindness. "Nurse" Mae Howell also was a memorable woman, being ready to attend to the ills, pains, or injuries of the students.

Of course, there were other staff members who were also very competent and dedicated. It is with great nostalgia that I reflect upon my service for the Lord and to those with whom I had the privilege to serve in Jamaica. Many of them have now passed to their earthly rest, but I certainly look forward to meeting them in the future kingdom.

Ordination to the Gospel Ministry

1971

WHEN my twin brother Russell and I were boys, frequently our Mother had encouraged us to look to the possibility of training for the pastoral ministry. We had no interest in the ministry. Our father was a very prominent church elder and lay preacher, and we would sit in awe as boys and youth, marveling at his ability to present the Word of God. Yet, we never aspired to follow in his footsteps. Indeed we were so afraid of doing any speaking in public that we never dreamed that one day both of us would be called to the gospel ministry.

Eventually we both decided to train as teachers at Avondale College, believing that we did not need to be as "good" to be teachers as to be pastors. Of course, this was an extraordinary misunderstanding of the holy calling to teach children and youth in a Christian school environment. When I was called to be the academic dean at West Indies College it never entered my head that one day I would be called into the gospel ministry. I served in that responsibility for less than six months before the West Indies College board voted to ask me to be the new college president to succeed Elder Vaz. It was something I had never expected because for a number of years all the presidents had been black West Indians. It seemed that the day of foreign white leadership—which had been continuous from the college's foundation in 1919 up until the early 1960s—had passed away at the time Jamaica was granted its independence from Great Britain. Thus the call to lead West Indies College was quite a surprise, and I saw it as an extraordinarily heavy responsibility especially for a 36-year-old. There has not been another non-West Indian president subsequent to my presidency.

I had not been in Jamaica long before being inspired to participate in an evangelistic crusade. Shortly after arriving in Jamaica, Elder H.S. Walters, the union president, conducted a very successful crusade in the capital city of Kingston. Cheryl and I attended these meetings a couple of times, and on one of those occasions I participated in the service. However, I, too, had a burden to be involved in evangelistic outreach, and I conducted, with a number of college students, a crusade less than two miles from the college campus. The venue was a shed with only one wall.

Of course, in the tropical climate of Jamaica this open-air location was not a disadvantage. In fact it was a great advantage because the weather was relatively warm for most of the year. Although Mandeville is situated at more than 2,000 feet above sea level, it was also warm for most of the year. Furthermore, there was no electricity in the area and therefore no air conditioning or even fans.

Much of the advertising was by word of mouth, though we also had printed simple advertising invitations. Come the people did, and each night we had a goodly number of attendees not of our faith. We had the privilege at the conclusion of the crusade to have about 20 people baptized in what was quite a sparsely populated area.

Not long after this crusade, I was approached by Elder Walters, telling me that the Union personnel believed that I should be ordained to the gospel ministry. While it is not unusual for senior college presidents to be ordained, somehow it had not crossed my mind until I was approached by Elder Walters. It brought a great sobering effect upon me. I had always believed that the ministry was a most sacred and holy calling. I realized, at least in part, what it would mean if I were to become an ordained representative of the Lord in His ministry.

Earlier in my life, at the age of 20, I had been ordained a deacon and at the age of 27 an elder. Yet to me the ordination to the worldwide ministry of the Seventh-day Adventist Church was a far greater responsibility, and I felt greatly humbled by this prospect. I thought of all the times my mother had been burdened that her boys become part of the gospel ministry. She, of course, was pleased that at the time both of her twin sons were serving the Lord overseas—my brother, Russell, in medical work in Southeast Asia and I in the educational work. I believe by this time her thoughts about either of us becoming ordained ministers had dimmed significantly, but she was gratified to know that we were in the service of God. I recall well the meeting I had with the union committee as they asked a series of questions. I indicated how unworthy I felt to be called by the Lord, through the brethren, to this holy responsibility. I could not accept that responsibility without seeking to fulfill the fullness of that calling in addition to my educational ministry.

Eventually the day for the ordination arrived. It was conducted not at the college nor even in Mandeville, but in Montego Bay, the largest city on the north coast of Jamaica. Another candidate, Pastor Sams, was ordained with me. He was later to become president of the Quebec Conference in Canada for quite a number of years. At this time he was ministering in the West Jamaica Conference where Montego Bay is located. Two major participants joined Jamaican church officials in the ordination service—Elder Bender Archibold, the then president of the Inter-American Division, and Dr. Charles Hirsch, the then General Conference Director of Education, who read the ordination vows.

I will never forget the import as I listened, in front of a packed congregation, to those five verses which were read to me on that occasion. Often, to this day, I think back to that ordination pledge I solemnly affirmed before all the witnesses. It will be helpful for the reader also to contemplate this vow, for in reality every faithful Seventh-day Adventist is called to follow these principles not necessarily in the fullest sense of an ordained minister, but in the area of his or her talents and calling.

> I charge thee therefore before God, and the Lord Jesus Christ, who shall judge the quick and the dead at his appearing and his kingdom; preach the word; be instant in season, out of season; reprove, rebuke, exhort with all longsuffering and doctrine. For the time will come when they will not endure sound doctrine; but after their

own lusts shall they heap to themselves teachers, having itching ears; and they shall turn away their ears from the truth, and shall be turned unto fables. But watch thou in all things, endure afflictions, do the work of an evangelist, make full proof of thy ministry. 2 Timothy 4:1–5

The Day the Mountain Shook

Jamaica, 1971

WHEN Cheryl and I arrived in Jamaica at the end of January 1970, we spent some time in a home which was always meant to be temporary until a home closer to the campus became available. For these first few months, as I explained earlier, we lived next door to the then president of the college, Elder Kenneth Vaz.

On the other side our neighbors were from the south Caribbean area. Elder Lashley was from Barbados and his wife from Guyana. They had come to West Indies College so that Elder Lashley could complete his baccalaureate degree which had not been available when he graduated from Caribbean Union College in Trinidad years before. With them were their children, the oldest being a son, Sylvan Lashley. Sylvan was then an academy student and a very fine young man. He stayed on when his parents returned to Barbados, and after graduating from the academy he became a college student and ultimately graduated from West Indies College. Later he was to become president of Caribbean Union College and, subsequently, president of Atlantic Union College.

However, by the summer a home had become available much closer to the campus—indeed in short walking distance—and we were able to relocate. It was a fine home of cinderblock construction reinforced with rebar simply because Jamaica was occasionally hit by earthquakes and devastating hurricanes. The most famous earthquake in the seventeenth century occurred at Port Royal, located on a peninsula close to the capital, Kingston, and located very close to where the present Norman Washington Manley International Airport is located. With that earthquake huge changes came in the contours of that region, and a remarkable situation occurred. A man was sucked down by one of the great convulsions into the depth of the ocean, only to be thrown up again by another upheaval. He lived to tell the story. Therefore, from time to time, there were some concerns either about a hurricane which was developing in the region or the possibility of another earth tremor or worse—earthquake. Thus all major homes were built with not only cinderblock but with strong fortification of rebar. The home we were living in was no exception. It was commodious, in fact more than my wife and I really needed, considering that at that time we had no children. We certainly were very comfortable in the home, and it allowed us frequently to host students or other guests for meals and fellowship.

At this time my wife was also serving in the college as my secretary. One particular morning around nine o'clock, I was sitting in my office carrying on the required duties of that day while Cheryl was in the next office, when a huge explosion rocked the mountainside on which the college was established. All the buildings on the campus were shaken by the explosion. Immediately the classrooms cleared as students and staff sought to find out the cause of the explosion. I also quickly hastened out and was shocked to see huge billows of smoke coming out of the home where we lived. We did not know whether or not a bomb had exploded in the home. It caused a great amount of alarm, but before many moments had passed a whole army of students were down at the house investigating what had taken place. I wondered that, if it was a bomb, there might be another one which might also explode. Of course I carefully made my way down there. My first thought was for the cat we had, Kippie. I knew that, if she was anywhere near the explosion she would be dead, but later we found her alive. Obviously she was not near the center of the explosion, but no doubt she was greatly alarmed by it.

Eventually we found the cause of the explosion. It was a hot water heater which had exploded. Apparently it had malfunctioned, and the huge pressure which built up inside had caused an unbelievably destructive explosion. The side wall was blown out, rebar and all, enough for a single-decker bus literally to drive through it. Much of the roof had exploded and some of the metal sheets were found on the roof of our neighbors' house. As the water heater was in a room next to the kitchen, the damage to the kitchen was devastating. Most of the cutlery was scattered around and, even worse, the china and glasses were almost all broken as the wall had caved in with the explosion. Our washing basket had been in the room where the water heater was located. We found much of the clothing in the rafters. Indeed, amazingly, some were between the rafters. It seems that as the clothes were thrown up, one rafter had gone up and then come down upon the clothes. It was a scene of great devastation. Of course, it was quickly realized that this could be dangerous because thieves and pilferers could easily find access to our house.

The maintenance staff rapidly blocked the area most devastated. Fortunately our sleeping quarters on the other side of the house were not seriously damaged, and we could eat in our dining room which also had to double for a kitchen for several months before the repairs to the house could be completed. I had no thought that such an explosion could be so violent. Cheryl and I contemplated the providence of God in saving our lives. If it had happened an hour and a half earlier, while we were eating breakfast, almost certainly we would have been killed. It is always possible to repair a broken building, but it is not possible for man to bring back to life someone who has been killed.

The people at the college rallied around us and helped us quickly to obtain some new cutlery, chinaware and glasses and other items which were damaged or destroyed in the explosion. Indeed, the outpouring of help was very moving to us. We were grateful for the wonderful love of our Jamaican brethren and sisters.

"I Don't Believe You"

1971

ONE Sabbath I was asked to give a short talk between Sabbath School and church service at the Central Jamaica camp meeting held in Spanish Town. I had pondered what I could say which would make an impact upon the people.

From the time I had arrived in Jamaica I was quite concerned about the fact that except for a very tiny number of people, all the Seventh-day Adventists were consumers of flesh food. It is true that the poor ate very little flesh because of their lack of money; however, even they ate flesh foods when it was available to them. Curried goat was a delicacy very popular in Jamaica. Cheryl and I attended only one Seventh-day Adventist wedding where curried goat was not the main attraction at the wedding feast following the service. Even poor families provided curried goat at a marriage feast. A number of Jamaicans told me that I didn't understand the cravings they had for flesh. I told them that Christ was well able to give them the victory. Jamaica, like most tropical countries, has an abundance of fruit, nuts, legumes, and vegetables well suited to a vegan diet.

Another traditional food for Jamaicans was ackee and salt fish (cod fish). Most readers have probably not heard of ackee. To me it is one of the most wonderful foods God ever created. Even though it will grow well in any tropical location, only two countries of the world seem to use it freely—Jamaica and Antigua, a tiny island nation in the Caribbean with an area of 170 square miles and a population of 69,000. Ackee grows on a medium sized tree with dark green, shiny leaves. In its fruiting season it produces a bell-shaped fruit which is rich red, giving the tree the appearance of the colors often seen at Christmas time. It is a very attractive sight. However, the covering of the fruit is leathery in texture and relatively thick. Once the fruit has matured the bell opens, revealing three large, black, shiny seeds at the end of three cream-colored soft, fleshy segments. This fruit is not sweet; in fact, it is used as a savory. The fleshy segments are cut away from the shining seeds and are mashed into what looks in a pan like scrambled eggs—a similar texture and color; however, it has its own unique flavor. We found it absolutely irresistible when cooked with tomato and onion. However the Jamaicans love to have it with cod fish. We were often assured that we could not leave Jamaica without at least trying ackee with cod fish. However, we managed to depart the country without ever succumbing to such suggestions that certainly had no appeal to us.

Unfortunately every year there were those who died of ackee poisoning. From what I could understand, if the pods are forced open then they are dangerous. Apparently cyanide gas is trapped within the pod and thus it is essential to wait until the pod has opened wide which allows the cyanide gas to escape and thus renders the fruit safe to eat.

I was deeply concerned at the amount of flesh consumed by most ministers. One very notable exception, as I have stated before, was Pastor Kenneth Vaz and his wife, both of whom were vegetarians. Almost all other ministers I knew were flesh consumers. I was very disappointed to find flesh being consumed in large quantities by ministers on special occasions.

If ever I had a desire to eat meat it certainly vanished in Jamaica. Many animals were butchered in the paddock and it was a sickening sight if we came across an animal being butchered as we drove by. In the markets we could see animal heads hanging on hooks with flies swarming around the meat. It was more than I could behold. The same was true at the fish markets where flies were inevitably all over the fish.

A notable occasion was held at the conclusion of the Bahamas Conference Constituency session. The incumbent president had been reelected, and the Conference held a banquet in an expensive tourist hotel for the ministers who had attended the session. As a minister and a delegate, I was invited to be there. To say the least it was disappointing to see the variety of meat—from chicken to fish to various cuts of red meat—which dominated the offerings. They had arranged for small quantities of vegetarian food to be there also. To the best of my observation I was the only one to eat the vegetarian food. Of course, there were those ministers who tried to make fun of the situation, "We better not get near Standish. He might see what we are eating." I tried to ignore such statements, hoping that my witness would have an impact upon some and also knowing that there was a level of conviction of guilt among some of these pastors over their indulgence in the "flesh pots of Egypt." While vegetarianism is not common among Seventh-day Adventists in Jamaica today, nevertheless there are increasing numbers of Jamaicans who have accepted the health message and use no flesh for which I thank the Lord. There are also increasing numbers of vegans.

At the Central Jamaican camp meeting I decided to address the issue of flesh foods. I began by asking a question, "How many of you believe that the Lord is coming soon?" The hands exploded all over that large congregation. I then leaned into the microphone and said softly, "I don't believe you." It was clear the people were shocked. They had no thought that would be my response to their sincere affirmation of belief. Then I quoted from the Spirit of Prophecy:

> Among those who are waiting for the coming of the Lord, meat eating will eventually be done away; flesh will cease to form a part of their diet. *Counsels on Diet and Foods*, pp. 380–381

I paused. You could have heard a pin drop. Then there was a soft whisper among the people.

I then proceeded to present a short talk on why we would be much better in health and spiritual life if we were vegetarians. At the conclusion the union president came to the front and with a great smile on his face he said, "Well, you can see that the doctor is very convicted on this issue." Nothing more was said. However, I pray that the little which I did say would have brought a sober realization to God's people.

It is very sad to know that many who profess faith in the three angels' messages and who claim to be longing for the return of Jesus are still ignoring this counsel. Sister White makes it plain that it is not a sin to eat clean meats; however, it is plain that no one who continues to eat flesh will be among the living saints, the 144,000, at the return of Jesus. All flesh eating will have been laid aside.

> Meat should not be placed before our children. Its influence is to excite and strengthen the lower passions, and has a tendency to deaden the moral powers. Grains and fruits prepared free from grease, and in as natural a condition as possible, should be the food for the tables of all who claim to be preparing for translation to heaven. *Testimonies for the Church*, vol. 2, p. 352.

> Those who have received instruction regarding the evils of the use of flesh foods, tea, and coffee, and rich and unhealthful food preparations, and who are determined to make a covenant with God by sacrifice, will not continue to indulge their appetite for food that they know to be unhealthful. God demands that the appetite be cleansed, and that self-denial be practiced in regard to those things which are not good. This is a work that will have to be done before His people can stand before Him a perfected people. *Testimonies for the Church*, vol. 9, p. 153–154.

Not too long after I came to West Indies College they had what was an annual feature of the college program—a recreation day at a chosen site. I was quite surprised that on that day the staff and students were permitted to bring flesh for eating during that recreation day. This seemed so out of place. At the college the diet was ovo-lacto vegetarian; no flesh was served. This seemed wholly inconsistent with the standards of the college, and I raised the question with the president, Elder Vaz, who himself was a vegetarian. He told me it had been a tradition long before he was there, and it was a feature very much looked forward to by the students. I told him that I could not in any way endorse such a lowering of the standards, even for one "special day."

As I made enquiries about the flesh served, I found that not infrequently staff members would invite students home for meals at which time they would serve flesh as a treat for the students. Those who served flesh were very popular. When the following year progressed toward this recreation day, I was now president of the college. I believed I had a responsibility and though against some moderate opposition and resistance, I banned all flesh from the food prepared for that day. That continued while I was president. I have no idea whether it continued after my presidency. I also made a strong plea to the staff who were inviting students to their homes not to serve flesh foods to them. Indeed, I made a plea that they deeply consider putting all flesh out of their diet. The Jamaican ladies were excellent cooks and were able to provide delicious meals quite independent of the use of flesh foods.

Death Threats

1971

THE violent crime rate in Jamaica was extraordinarily high. Indeed, the Jamaican *Gleaner*, which was the national morning newspaper, reported while we were in Jamaica that violent crime was twelve times that of the United States per ratio of the population. This led to constant reports of brutal or impulsive murders which took place around the nation. While there were pockets of crime areas where the incident of crime was more likely, nevertheless, there seemed to be no place where murder was not likely to occur, even in very rural situations. Part of the reason, I suspect, was the fact that almost all country people, especially men, carry machetes. Machetes are used for many useful purposes—cutting bunches of banana, cutting grass, or perhaps necessary trimming. It was a natural part of life for country men to carry their machete with them. Thus if two men engaged in a violent argument, it was possible that in the flurry of the dispute one would cut the other with a machete, leading either to grievous injury or, not uncommonly, death.

It was not unusual to read a story in the *Gleaner* which would report something like this, "A fuss ensued and the deceased was allegedly cut on the neck by the machete of the suspect." However there were other violent crimes which were associated with robberies. While there were many affluent Jamaicans, there was also a great deal of poverty, and this led to much stealing. Sometimes, however, in the act of stealing someone was killed—maybe someone who had heard noises in his home or maybe someone who resisted the robber's attempt to steal. For example, there was an Australian couple living in Kingston. One Friday night they had been at a movie house. On their way home, a Jamaican snatched the bag of the wife while they were walking along the sidewalk (footpath). The husband called out angrily after him, and the thief shot the husband dead. This caused quite a deal of fear with my inlaws when, on the Sabbath morning, a neighbor came excitedly to report that she had read in the newspaper that an unnamed Australian had been shot dead in Kingston. Of course, the only Australians in Jamaica which my inlaws knew were Cheryl and me. By the grace of God nothing like this happened to us. Thank God for the protection of His angels!

One of the most publicized deaths took place during a robbery of a Seventh-day Adventist Church. It was a church in which I had preached and on another occasion had helped conduct a funeral. This happened not long after we had left Jamaica. During the church service two men came to rob the tithes and offerings which had just been collected. As the robbers were running out of the church, the second man was tripped by one of the members. Of course, there was a hastening to alert the police but when the police arrived the thief was dead. Apparently the church member pummeled him so hard that he died. This, I thought, was a sad commentary upon the members of the Trenchtown Church in West Kingston.

On two occasions I was close to acts of larceny. One Sunday afternoon my wife and I were shopping at the supermarket in Mandeville. When we heard a scream, we saw a middleaged white lady and a man running from her with her handbag. The cry went up, "Thief" from the sparse number of witnesses. Two men asked whether I would try to help them catch the thief. I told them to get in the back seat of the car as I drove in the direction of where the thief had run. Eventually we came side by side with the thief, and the men jumped out, but he quickly ran down the embankment and into the woods. However, the men—one of whom proved to be an offduty policeman—told me where to go where they believed they could cut off his retreat. We quickly drove to the spot, and not far ahead there was a man starting to count the money. When he saw the men he ran again. I waited for the two men to return. When they returned they returned empty handed. I asked what had happened and their simple answer was, "Bad dogs." In other words they were afraid of the guard dogs which were aroused by the chase. The thief, with much more at stake, continued on his way and evaded capture. He was never apprehended.

When we returned to the shopping mall a senior police officer was there, and he asked what had happened. We explained to him. He was quite upset with me that I had not run the thief down when I had the opportunity. However, this was something my conscience would not allow me to do even though I would dearly have desired to see the man apprehended.

On another occasion, one night I was in Kingston, and in the dim light a police officer was leading what looked like about a 14-year-old youth. The youth was bleeding fairly freely. Others who saw the situation cried out to the policeman, "What him done?" The policeman shouted back, "Larceny." Then a number of them cried out, " 'im deserve it, 'im deserve it," meaning he deserved the obvious roughing up that the policeman had given to him. Sometimes I felt that though the people in Jamaica were very religious, some of them seemed to have no compunction concerning robbery.

There were a number of times when there were extremely dangerous situations. I was attending a Union committee meeting when an urgent telephone call came for me telling me simply, "Come quickly, they are going to kill Mr. Green." Mr. Green was the farm manager at West Indies College. I had no idea what the situation was, but I had no alternative but to go back to discover what I could do to save what was obviously a very dangerous situation. It was only a half-mile drive up the hill, and when I drove through the gates there was Mr. Green with three men from the nearby community. They were engaged in violent shouting at one another all in the patois language. I discovered in Jamaica, even for the educated class, when one became angry it was always expressed not in English but in patois. Apparently the words seemed more cutting in patois. I also found that Jamaicans found jokes told in patois far funnier than those told in English.

I could see this situation was serious. All men had their machetes with them, including Mr. Green. So violent and so rapid was their patois talk that, though I could understand a reasonable amount of patois by this time, I could not determine what the real issue was. So I walked toward the four men, while not proceeding so close that I was in range of the machetes. With a commanding voice, I called out, "What's going on here?" All four men started to shout together. I stopped them, "Let me first hear from Mr. Green, and I want you men to be quiet. Then I will give you the opportunity to tell me your side of the story." Mr. Green told me that he had found these men stealing wood off our campus, and he was protecting the interest of the college. I would much rather have a farm manager than a few pieces of firewood; however, I knew that he was very sincere in what he was doing.

I asked the men for their story while requesting Mr. Green to keep quiet. It was about the same. They were just needing wood for cooking. Eventually I was able to calm down both sides of the equation and I gave instruction to both Mr. Green and to the men, "If you really need some wood from the campus, we are not going to deprive you of that wood. However, there is wood which would be more appropriate for you to take and other wood which we need. So, from now on, if you need wood you come to Mr. Green and ask him to show you which wood you can take and which wood you cannot take." It was such an easy solution, yet the tempers were such that there was definitely the possibility of a much worse outcome to the situation.

On another occasion an academy student had been involved in a moral situation. She was a 15-year-old girl from a parish (county) between the college and Kingston. It was always the policy of West Indies College to drive home anyone who had been expelled from either the academy or college. Rarely did I have this responsibility, but as I was traveling a little later that day with my wife to Kingston, I took the responsibility. As we approached closer to her home the girl started to whimper and say, "My daddy will kill me, my daddy will kill me." I told her I would be there to explain everything to her father, but the closer we got to her home, the greater the fear was expressed by this frightened girl. We parked the car and walked quite a distance to the little, humble dwelling where the girl's family lived in the countryside of Jamaica.

As we arrived the mother saw us and intuitively knew something had gone wrong with her daughter, and she started to cry. I explained to her as kindly as I could what had taken place. The mother said, "Her father will kill, her father will kill her." Now I knew I was dealing with "an ignorant man" (a dangerous man). I told the mother I would wait there until the father came home. This I did. When, as carefully as possible, I began to explain to the father what had happened, he immediately lost complete control of himself against his foolish daughter and went to where his machete was hanging. I knew what that meant. I called the girl to run with me, and, with my wife, I quickly got her in the back seat of the car, and my wife and I drove off before the father could reach us. I had no alternative but to take her to the home of the pastor of the church they attended.

The response of the minister was not helpful when he learned the situation. The teenager, who was already in a state of great emotional distress, not only because of the disgrace of being dismissed from West Indies College Academy but because of the response of her father, needed much more fatherly advice and encouragement to turn away from those sins of the past than the castigating she received from the pastor. The pastor told her that he was absolutely embarrassed by what she had done, that he had written a good recommendation for her to attend West Indies College, now the college will never have any confidence in his recommendations. So the poor girl had to suffer a verbal roasting from the minister. However, the pastor and his wife did agree to keep her until it was safe to send her back to her home.

There was another serious threat which was made while I was president of West Indies College. A young man who had become a disciplinary problem in his senior year at the West Indies College Academy was not allowed to graduate. The reason was that not only did students have to pass the necessary examinations but they had also to show themselves to be of good moral and spiritual character. This young man, while passing his exams, had failed to measure up spiritually. However, he had American residency, and therefore not long after he finished high school he was back in the United States and was drafted into the American army during the Vietnam War. After some training he was assigned to go to Vietnam. Before he left he returned to Jamaica. He was still seething over the fact that he had not received his high school diploma, and he sent warnings around that he was coming to West Indies College to shoot some of the leaders. His comment was a simple one, "I'm going to die in Vietnam, so if I get hanged here in Jamaica it will make no difference." He was referring to the fact that hanging was the means of execution for murderers in Jamaica. By the grace of God, he did not carry out the threats, though they were somewhat unsettling.

As a footnote he did go to Vietnam and survived it and eventually came back to Jamaica and married one of the finest girls we had had at West Indies College. I felt very uncomfortable with the fact that this girl had agreed to marry this young man.

On another occasion, my wife and I were traveling in Kingston. I have forgotten now what had taken us at night to West Kingston, the most dangerous spot in Jamaica. We were having trouble with our car. While it was only a minor trouble, it always necessitated getting out of the car, lifting the hood, and making minor adjustments before the car would start again. The last thing which we wanted was to get out of the car in a place like West Kingston, especially at night, because murders were frequent and it was always believed that it was not a safe place for white people to spend much time.

But it happened. While in West Kingston the car stopped. There were people walking around. We had no idea who they were or what kind of people they were but I had no alternative but to seek to fix the problem so we could continue on our journeying away from this area. You can understand that there was much prayer. By the grace of God my wife and I were protected. I was able to get the car started and we made a rapid exit into more friendly territory of the city.

One of the most remarkable experiences happened in relation to a young academy student. Identical twin brothers came to the academy from Bermuda. Their much older half-brother was a fine young man, studying for the ministry. He had been chosen a resident student monitor in the young men's dormitory. Soon the college dean of men began to notice the frequent absences of one of the twins. In a determined effort to keep this 16-year-old from wandering off, he strongly restricted the youth's activities and kept a close watch on him. What the dean did not know was that to obtain a little money this boy had come in contact with some of the ganga (marijuana) operators. He had been disappearing to go on journeys into the country to bring back bags of ganga which were being flown out of Jamaica in the middle of the night from the airstrip located close by the West Indies Union office.

However, now he was unable to do this, and the men who were relying upon his services became very angry and threatened to kill him if he did not continue to serve them. He tried to explain to them the situation, and these men decided that they would take drastic action against the college. They focused upon the young men's dormitory—a wooden structure, and decided to burn it down in the middle of the night. At the time, we were in the process of building a new cinderblock dormitory, but it had not been completed ready for occupancy. If that building had been lit there would have been terrible carnage in lives because, by any kind of evaluation, the building was fire unsafe. Only the grace of God kept this dormitory from being a death trap. These men were determined to burn it down no matter what happened, but they had not taken into account the protective angels of the Lord.

As they were driving up the hill to the college, all four tires flattened. Yet still determined to carry out their wicked plan, they left the car and walked to the back side of the campus close to where Cheryl and I lived. There they began to climb up the steep embankment when suddenly a search light came upon them. Believing that the search light was from the college, they hastened to the other end and started to climb the campus, yet once again a search light forced them to stop and eventually give up on their murderous plan. We had no doubt that "the angel of the Lord encampeth round about them that fear him, and delivereth them" (Psalm 34:7). We had no doubt that God had worked a miracle to save the lives of the young men in the men's dormitory. Every day we are safe in the arms of Jesus, and we have faith in the protection of the holy angels. In this wicked world we can rest in peace. For his own protection we returned the youth home to Bermuda.

New Challenges in Jamaica

1971–1972

I HAVE said many times, I received ten years' experience while serving about three and one-half years in Jamaica. There were difficulties there which I have not had to deal with in other parts of the world—difficulties which had to be addressed though they were difficult to handle. Here is a sample of those difficulties.

We were located more than 2,000 feet above sea level. Of course, it was a beautiful climate as we were at elevation in the tropics. It was almost the perfect climate—warm but not hot in the summer and cool but not cold in the winter. Summer was the wet season, and in winter it was the dry season, as is usually the case in the tropics. Thus during the winter we had terrible problems with the water supply. There was a large collection system for water which filled up our large water tanks. But even with the most careful usage of water during the winter months we were likely to have times when there was no water. I asked the management of one of the Bauxite Companies, who themselves had to drill for water, if they would come to the college to evaluate our water situation with the view that they might be able to help us. The manager of this Bauxite Company came with his chief hydrologist to make an evaluation. The evaluation of the hydrologist was very discouraging. He believed that we probably would have to sink a well at least down to sea level. The cost would be prohibitive, and the pump needed to lift the water about half a mile from sea level was out of the question.

Thus we had no alternative but to bring in large water tankers from the lowlands to ease the needs from time to time. It was always difficult when water ran out during the evening. I would soon have a group of students at my door to tell me water was needed. We could do nothing at night because the tankers were not operating, and each time I would have to tell them that the first thing in the morning we would make sure that water was brought up. As you can imagine, this was a very costly operation for a college which was so financially strapped. It was common for the college to be at least 80,000 Jamaican dollars in debt—at that time the equivalent of 100,000 U. S. dollars—a huge amount in the economy of Jamaica in the early 1970s. It was always very difficult for the business manager and the treasurer as they sought to balance the outflow with the income.

Because of the situation in Jamaica, West Indies College was not unique in its difficulty of paying bills, and therefore businesses were slow to stop offering credit to the college because they knew at least eventually they would obtain the funds albeit maybe six months or so after the debt had been incurred. They were not so certain of obtaining money from other debtors.

One night I was awakened about one o'clock in the morning when the dean of women had discovered that one of the girls in the dormitory was missing. We were able to raise a number of students to help us seek to find this girl. However, I was anxious to find the student assigned as the night watchman for that evening. I hoped he could give us some idea of what might have happened to the young lady or what he had seen which might help us in the investigation. Maybe someone had come to pick her up and drive her away. But search as we may we could not find the night watchman until eventually we found him in an educational department class room watching television. I was aghast that a young man paid to be a security guard during the night would spend his time watching television. I immediately removed him from the position, which greatly angered him, and for the rest of my stay at West Indies College he refused to speak to me and always looked with a hostile countenance whenever he saw me. Yet years later, when I returned to Jamaica, I met that young man, now an accountant, at the Union Office. He came to apologize to me for what he had done and for his attitude toward me. He said, "I knew you did the only thing you could have done." It was not until the next day that the young lady was found. She had gone off campus, and the college had to take suitable actions against her.

There is no question that most of the students were very fine young people. However from time to time a volatility would be created by an incident developing into a serious activation. One lunch time I had taken an officer from a bank with which the college had an account, to eat with us in the cafeteria. While we were eating, the cafeteria director, Sister Nembhard, the wife of the Union Secretary, a Bahamian by birth, came to me quite concerned to report that the students were saying, "The peas are stink." She was referring to the gungu peas, more like beans, which were a common staple protein part of the Jamaican diet. They were delicious. So the claim was that they were bad. The report soon spread around the students and they became hostile. I asked Mrs. Nembhard to bring the leaders of the complaint and I accompanied them to the kitchen. There was a large aluminum pot containing the gungu peas. I asked Mrs. Nembhard whether the peas which the students had eaten had come from that same pot. She affirmed that it was the only pot containing the peas. So I asked her to put some in a bowl and in the presence of these students I started to eat them. They were fine. There was nothing tainted about them. So I told the students that the peas were fine and there was no need to be concerned about them. However, it developed into a large scale rebellion during the afternoon as word was spread that the students were being asked to eat "stink peas," meaning peas that had gone rancid. Some threw food and even plates and utensils around the cafeteria after I had left. I returned to the cafeteria and read the "riot act" to the culprits. They stopped their vandalism, but it did not solve the issue.

It became such an issue that I was compelled to call a special chapel meeting for all the students that night. I prayed earnestly what I would say to try to stop the developing incident. After some introductory remarks explaining to the students this was not a civilized way to handle concerns, I then asked all the students who had eaten the gungu peas at lunch to stand. About one third of the students stood. I then asked, "How many of you have had stomach aches or have become sick since then?" I did not wait long because I did not want some to imagine that he or she might have had a reaction. There was no response. Then I told the students that I did not want to hear anymore about the peas. Indeed that was the end of the situation.

One last experience taught me a very important lesson. West Indies College had very strict dress codes, which included that no student could be on the college campus with the tail of his shirt hanging out. This was a common way to dress by some of the youth of Jamaica, as well as other countries, but it was certainly in bad taste for those training for the work of God. One morning a community student was walking toward the chapel. I noted that his shirt was out. My response to him was, "You are a wretch." Little did I understand the significance of the word "wretch" in Jamaica. The comment obviously shook the young man. In Australia, quite commonly people in a light hearted, or at least not in a demeaning way will call someone a "wretch." But I was to learn that the word "wretch" was about the worst word which I could call an individual. I often wondered what the reaction of Jamaicans was when they read Romans 7:24 and Revelation 3:17.

> O wretched man that I am! who shall deliver me from the body of this death? Romans 7:24
>
> Because thou sayest, I am rich, and increased with goods, and have need of nothing; and knowest not that thou art wretched, and miserable, and poor, and blind, and naked. Revelation 3:17

I believe they have an understanding far deeper than many from other parts of the English-speaking world. Within the hour the student's father was in my office, absolutely aghast that the president of West Indies College would use such degrading language to his son. I was very thankful that this man was a converted Christian because if he had been unconverted he could have taken violent action against me. However, that was not the intent of this man. He wanted to understand how a president could use such a degrading word about his son. I humbly asked his forgiveness and explained to him that the meaning of the word to me was much different from that which it obviously was to him. By God's grace we were able to become good friends and I know that he respected me greatly before I left the appointment as president of the college.

Voodoo

Haiti, 1971

HAITI is famous—or should I more appropriately say infamous—for its voodoo. Haiti is a fascinating nation. It has the honor of being the first predominantly black nation to shake off colonial rule and become an independent nation. This it did in 1804 when the French Colonial government was overthrown. Yet Haiti is a poverty stricken nation. It is listed among the 25 poorest nations in the world. In spite of this, it has many vibrant citizens and many faithful Seventh-day Adventists members.

In the summer of 1971 Haiti was the first stop for my wife and me on our preaching itinerary through the islands of the Caribbean, which ended on the north coast of South America in the former British colony of Guyana. We were privileged to have a very fine Seventh-day Adventist to show us around Port-au-Prince, Haiti's capital. Brother Toussant was an official in the national postal service. He spent time with us and showed us a little of the beautiful mountain regions behind the capital city of Port-au-Prince.

At the time of our visit, Haiti was still reeling from the effects of many years of dictatorship by the man who was call Papa Doc. Papa Doc had ruled Haiti with ruthlessness, and untold numbers of people had lost their lives who dared to express even what would seem the slightest opposition to his iron-fisted control of this poverty-devastated nation. Papa Doc had died not long before we arrived there. Before his death he had insured that his son—a rather obese individual unlike his father—would be his successor. The son still quite young, known as Baby Doc, clearly had not the same shrewd political control of his father, and eventually he would be disposed and exiled from the country. But that happened subsequent to our visit to Haiti.

I had been scheduled to speak in a very large auditorium, and each night it was packed with eager listeners. I was especially blessed with a good translator. I was fascinated by the fact that all those who knew at least some English crowded into the front seats in their eagerness to improve their English and occasionally help the translator when he was struggling for a word. Almost all the educated people speak French, though Creole is spoken far and wide in this country. Creole is a language which I am told is a mixture of African, French and perhaps other words and has little grammatical construction.

While we were there, however, there was torrential rain which led to serious flooding in the city of Port-au-Prince as the water cascaded down from the mountains behind the city. The standard of hygiene and sewage disposal was very poor in this financially strapped nation. For example, raw sewage was carried by open trenches even in many major residential areas of the city. The whole situation was greatly exacerbated by the flooding, resulting in much sewage being carried in the flood waters. I believe that this almost certainly contributed to the terrible illness which overtook me in our next destination—the Dominican Republic. However, I had no immediate ill effects during my ministries in Haiti.

Cheryl and I were greatly surprised when the leaders of the then called Franco-Haitian Union said they had arranged for us to visit a tourist place where voodoo demonstrations were provided for inquisitive tourists. This really shocked us. We had heard much about voodoo before coming to Haiti and knew that it was a religion deeply riveted in paganism and spiritism. Kindly we declined that invitation. The men were not a little surprised. They indicated that many ministers and leaders from the United States had attended such demonstrations. My only response was, "Well, each person has to make his own decision of what to do." I told the brethren that it was my practice not to put myself deliberately in any place where Satan's control and power would be demonstrated. I believe this is a lesson for all of us. We have a serious challenge to meet with the strength of Christ, all of the temptations and deceptions of Satan which come upon us, without deliberately attending places where we know his nefarious evil will be present. However, while in Port-au-Prince we could not avoid hearing every evening, just as the sun was setting, the rhythmic beating of the drums calling the devotees of this satanic ritual to attend this form of devil worship. How our hearts yearned for the myriads of people in Haiti who are wholly under the control of Satan and worship him rather than our loving God.

We discovered that in Haiti every time there is an evangelistic crusade the deacons are trained how to deal with people who manifest devil possession at the crusade. It would seem that rarely are the evangelistic crusades free from such devilish manifestations. Devil possession is so common in Haiti that attendees pay little attention to such manifestations. The deacons know that such individuals, be they male or female, be they old or young, have superhuman strength when under the devilish control of Satan, and it requires many deacons to remove such an individual from the crusade so that the spread of the everlasting gospel can continue. Satan does everything to disrupt the presence of Christ and His work in countries such as this. Clearly, again, we recognize that when we surrender our lives to Jesus, He liberates us and gives us the freedom that all true Christians have. However, those who surrender their lives to Satan are held in ironclad servitude and misery to the one who is the enemy of souls and the enemy of Christ.

> For the law of the Spirit of life in Christ Jesus hath made me free from the law of sin and death. Romans 8:2

13 I Wondered Whether I Would Die

The Dominican Republic, 1971

IN the summer of 1971, Cheryl and I had been authorized by the West Indies College board to make an itinerary to many of the islands of the Caribbeans, seeking to find those young people who might be interested in training for the service of God at West Indies College. The itinerary took us to Haiti, Dominican Republic, Puerto Rico, Anguilla, St. Martins, British Virgin Islands, American Virgin Islands, St. Kitts, Nevis, Antigua, Dominica, Martinique, Guadeloupe, St. Lucia, Grenada, St. Vincent, Barbados, Trinidad, Tobago and Guyana. It certainly was a fascinating experience to see these many island nations. A few of the islands were still colonies of Great Britain, but all had at one time been colonies of one European nation or another—Great Britain, France, Spain, Netherlands and Denmark. Some of them had changed hands many times. For example St. Lucia had changed thirteen times between the British and the French, the British "winning" the last time. However, most of the names on this island nation bespoke of their French occupation.

We first visited Haiti where God blessed our ministry, as we recounted in the previous chapter.

Then we proceeded to the Dominican Republic. The Dominican Republic shares the island of Hispaniola with Haiti. Haiti has approximately the western one third and the Dominican Republic the eastern two thirds. However, the Haitians speak French, and the Dominicans speak Spanish. It was an island off the coast of the Dominican Republic where Christopher Columbus first made landfall on his famous 1492 discovery of the new world.

We were met at the airport by Pastor Wesley Taylor, accompanied by his small son, also named Wesley. Pastor Taylor was an American who was ministering at this time in the Dominican Republic. He had been born in Bolivia where his physician father was ministering. Having grown up in a Latin-American environment, he spoke Spanish just as fluently as he spoke English. So that we would not miss him, he held up an issue of the *Review and Herald*, which we quickly recognized, and we were happy to meet a fellow minister who spoke English. We enjoyed the hospitality of their home during our stay in the Dominican Republic, and what a blessing it was!

That night I preached at one of the main churches in Santo Domingo, the capital city of the Dominican Republic. I had felt well and strong during the sermon; however, as I was shaking hands with the people as they departed from the church, I suddenly became terribly sick and had to excuse myself, for now I realized I had a high temperature, and I was suffering vomiting and diarrhea—all with no warning. What had caused it I could not be sure. However, I knew that it was most likely something I ate or drank in Haiti which was contaminated and now had given me a violent reaction. (I have visited the Dominican Republic six times since then without a hint of sickness.)

The Taylors did everything they could to make me comfortable and to reduce the fever. But the fever continued to rise until it had reached the danger point above 104 degrees—very high for an adult. They quickly sought professional help, and a Seventh-day Adventist nurse and a Roman Catholic doctor came to care for me and continued to do so until eventually I recovered. Even though they could not speak English and I could not speak Spanish, I felt the loving care of these people.

At the time, I felt so weak and sick I wondered whether I would die. I do not think I have ever had such a high temperature before or since. However, with the loving care of those in the Dominican Republic, I slowly recovered. This meant a rescheduling of our itinerary because I was next scheduled to preach at Mayaguez on the western side of Puerto Rico where the Antillean Union College is located and which is a stronghold of Seventh-day Adventism. However, I had to cancel that visit and continue the rest of my schedule down the Caribbean.

I was not to know at that time, but I was to have the privilege to work with Elder Wesley Taylor in the service of the Lord. While I was dean of the college at Weimar I invited him to become a teacher on our Bible faculty, which he did, where his son Wesley, a brilliant student, completed his baccalaureate degree. Later, in the second year of Hartland Institute, Elder Taylor was to transfer and he taught Bible at Hartland College for six years, most of which time he also pastored the Warrenton Church, about 40 miles north of Hartland. Both Pastor Taylor and his wife were very dedicated Christians and wonderful examples to the students attending the college.

My wife and I were later to become sick again on this journey, this time in Tobago. Both of us awakened with low level fever and feelings of weakness. We believe it was from water we had drunk in Trinidad. I had preached in Port of Spain, the capital city, and then we were taken by the educational director of the Caribbean Union further south to the city of San Fernando where I believe we both drank water which was to upset our stomachs.

An interesting feature of our visit to San Fernando was our first meeting with Dr. Ralph Larson and his wife Jean. Dr. Larson was then a professor of the religion department at Atlantic Union College, where he taught the practical areas of evangelism and homiletics. During that summer he was evangelizing in Trinidad. It was toward the end of his crusade, and the meeting for that day had just completed when we arrived so we had the opportunity to greet one another, but little were we to know that Ralph and his wife were to become very dear friends of ours later. Still today, though Jean has passed away, I still count Ralph and his second wife, Betty, as very dear and precious friends. It was Dr. Larson who nobly stood for the great truths of our faith when pastor at the Campus Hill Church in Loma Linda. He was to give the trumpet a certain sound when there were so many defectors from the faith and from those preaching truth and righteousness. While he was pastor there he invited a number of faithful pastors to preach at his church. I had the privilege to preach there several times, as did my twin brother Russell.

Dr. Larson stood when champions were few and where there were those who strongly opposed his staunch stand for salvation. He has written some fine books, perhaps the most important of which is *The Word Was Made Flesh*—a definitive work on the human nature of Christ showing that leaders of the Seventh-day Adventist Church have from the earliest times written declaring Christ had taken upon Himself our fallen nature, as the Bible and the Spirit of Prophecy unequivocally attest.

On one occasion, Dr. Larson had asked to speak with the North American Division Union Conference leaders at a meeting chaired by the Division president. He intended to explain to the union presidents the belief which he held concerning the human nature of Christ and the sure Word of Inspiration affirming the power of Christ to provide victorious Christian living. While he was waiting outside, he was flabbergasted to overhear one of the union presidents urging the division president not to waste their time by having Dr. Larson come to talk with them. There were a number of other presidents who seemed to acquiesce to this union president. Dr. Larson easily identified who that union president was because he knew him relatively well, and he recognized his distinctive southern accent.

The division president explained that he had promised Dr. Larson the opportunity to speak with them and therefore he must honor that promise. Dr. Larson entered and made it very plain that he had overheard what had taken place, and then he proceeded to do all he could to explain to these men the message which God had given to us for the preparation of a people to inherit the eternal kingdom. What impact his presentation made is not easy to evaluate, although one of those presidents boldly came out, strongly proclaiming support for the truth that Christ took upon Himself our fallen, sinful nature.

> For what the law could not do, in that it was weak through the flesh, God sending his own Son in the likeness of sinful flesh, and for sin, condemned sin in the flesh. Romans 8:3
>
> Forasmuch then as the children are partakers of flesh and blood, he also himself likewise took part of the

same; that through death he might destroy him that had the power of death, that is, the devil; and deliver them who through fear of death were all their lifetime subject to bondage. For verily he took not on him the nature of angels; but he took on him the seed of Abraham. Wherefore in all things it behoved him to be made like unto his brethren, that he might be a merciful and faithful high priest in things pertaining to God, to make reconciliation for the sins of the people. For in that he himself hath suffered being tempted, he is able to succour them that are tempted. Hebrews 2:14-18

For we have not an high priest which cannot be touched with the feeling of our infirmities; but was in all points tempted like as we are, yet without sin. Hebrews 4:15

It was in the order of God that Christ should take upon Himself the form and nature of fallen man. *Spiritual Gifts*, vol. 4a, p. 115

His human nature was created; it did not even possess angelic powers. It was human, identical to our own. . . . A human body and a human mind were His. *Selected Messages*, Book 3, p. 129

Clad in the vestments of humanity, the Son of God came down to the level of those He wished to save. In Him was no guile or sinfulness; He was ever pure and undefiled, yet He took upon Him our sinful nature. *Review and Herald*, December 15, 1896

But coming back to the sickness of my wife and I in Tobago. It was uncertain whether I would be able to speak that night. However, indeed while I was still feeling sick, I did take the service, and it was to a seemingly receptive congregation. Providentially the illness had gone for both of us by the next morning as we continued our journey back to Trinidad and then on to Guyana.

Face to Face With a Rebel Leader in Anguilla

Anguilla, 1971

DURING our itinerary in the Caribbean in July of 1971, I had the opportunity to preach on the tiny island of Anguilla. Anguilla is so small that most people in the world have never heard of it. Anguilla, a British colony, had a population of about 6,000 and is located in the northern part of the Caribbean Sea not far from the island of St. Martens, which is partly administered by France and partly by the Netherlands.

We flew into Anguilla on a small commuter flight from St. Martens. The landing strip was very primitive, and the immigrations customs office was located in a small shed, the only building associated with the airport. When we arrived there we found no one to meet us even though we had sent a letter some time before, announcing that we would be there and that I would be speaking to the people that night. However, to our surprise we were told that the Seventh-day Adventist pastor on the island had also landed on the same plane, so we quickly made contact with him. The pastor was surprised to see us. He knew nothing about our planned arrival, for he had been away for some time and therefore had not been home to receive the letter which we had sent.

He was very happy, however, to know of our visit and I explained that I was the president of West Indies College (now North Caribbean University) and was there to speak to the believers in Anguilla that night and to show a film of the college which had been aired on Jamaica national television. He said he would quickly gather the people together. Anguilla is such a tiny island that he was able to visit the homes of all the believers and announce our arrival and the plan for the meeting in the church that night.

During the meantime, we were taken for a tour around the island which took only a relatively short time. This island is a very flat island. Its claim to fame seemed to lie in two areas: a rather nice beach in one area of the island and the salt mines, the major industry on the island.

By the time we had reached Anguilla we were well into our itinerary which called for us to spend only one night before moving on to another location. We had visited Haiti and the Dominican Republic. We had spoken on the island of Tortilla (of the British Virgin Islands) and then on the islands of St. Croix and St. Thomas (of the American Virgin Islands). From there I had spoken in St. Kitts (Christopher) and its fellow island Nevis and St. Martens before we had flown to Anguilla.

I had explained to the pastor of Anguilla that I needed a film projector so that I could show the film of the West Indies College. He told me that that was going to be very difficult because there were very few projectors on the island of Anguilla. However, he would do his best.

After some time and making enquiries, he said there seemed to be only one person who had a film projector, and that was "Webster." "We will have to search for him to find out where he is." I had heard of the rebellion of Anguilla against the British government but did not know most of the details. I discovered the rebellion was led by this same man—Webster. I further learned that Webster was a Seventh-day Adventist who had been involved in the political process of the island. As you can imagine, the process was not very sophisticated with a population of only 6,000 and many less voters. He had eventually risen to the position of chief minister of the island nation, the equivalent to a prime minister of a much larger colonial nation. It was during his administration that the people became very dissatisfied with some of the administrative policies and actions of the British government, and under his leadership he and his council took action to declare independence from the British government.

The British quickly put down the rebellion. They sent in paratroopers to return the island to British rule. It was a bloodless action by the British, because the islanders knew that they had no hope of succeeding in military action with the British paratroopers. Thus British rule was restored, and order came back to this tiny nation.

However, soon thereafter, Webster left his position as chief minister. Sadly, by the time we had reached the island, he was no longer a member of the Seventh-day Adventist church, because he had been disfellowshipped for adultery. His wife and children, however, were still faithful members and attendees of the Seventh-day Adventist church.

Eventually the pastor found Webster at the home of a friend, and he agreed not only to loan the film projector, but also to attend the meeting and operate the projector. It was at the meeting that I met this rebel leader. He proved to be a friendly man and seemed interested in the message I preached and in the film of the West Indies College. However, the projector did not function well, and several times Webster had to stop the projector to try to improve its functioning. One thing stood out: Webster was a very determined man. He refused to give up when others would have probably given up. Through his persistence, the people were eventually able to see the whole film.

I had the opportunity to speak with Webster and encourage him to find his way back to the Lord and to the Seventh-day Adventist faith. I have no record of whether or not he did return to the Lord. His moment of glory was so short lived. I found in talking to others on the island that he was greatly disliked by many. His actions in leading the rebellion was an exercise in futility, certain to fail against the might of the British military. I could not but recall the words of Holy Scripture.

> For what is a man profited, if he shall gain the whole world, and lose his own soul? Or what shall a man give in exchange for his soul? Matthew 16:26

Death in the Hospital

Georgetown, Guyana, 1971

DURING our itinerary through the many islands of the Caribbean, Cheryl and I reached our most southerly point in Georgetown, the capital of Guyana. Guyana is located on the north coast of South America, though it is normally included in what was known as the British West Indies. It has a relatively sparse population, with East Indians in the majority and African blacks a large minority. Also, especially in the south, there are quite a few indigenous Indians. At times, this has caused significant political unrest. Georgetown itself is a gracious city with many quaint and beautiful colonial buildings. Being built on flat coastal land, it seems very vulnerable to any abnormal swelling of the tides. In fact, much of the city is just below sea level, and small dikes protect the city from the waves.

Flying from Port of Spain in Trinidad to Georgetown, Guyana, we met Dr. and Mrs. Neufeld on the plane. They were Canadians, and Dr. Neufeld had accepted a call to be a replacement physician at the Davis Memorial Hospital, the Seventh-day Adventist Hospital, in Georgetown. We were happy to meet these fellow believers on the flight, and as we were accommodated in an apartment building at the hospital we got to know them a little. I was there to present a series of meetings in the largest Seventh-day Adventist church in Georgetown.

However, we had been there barely a couple of days when Dr. Neufeld fell very ill and required hospitalization. He was diagnosed with a blockage in his intestines which demanded surgery almost immediately. Mrs. Neufeld was a trained nurse herself, and you can understand why she and the family were very alarmed. It was providential that on relief at the hospital was a very experienced surgeon, Dr. Lloyd Pratt, from Sacramento, California. Also at the hospital was a young Filipino doctor, Dr. Medina. After a heavy day of work in the hospital, the doctors and nursing staff had to commence this operation late that night. We stayed in the hospital waiting room with Sister Neufeld to offer whatever support we could give. As is the case in so many mission hospitals, the hospital was sorely understaffed. It especially lacked well-trained and experienced professionals. This added to the concern of Mrs. Neufeld. It is always more difficult when events like this take place when you are far from home. The situation was greatly complicated when an East Indian woman expecting her twelfth child, went into labor. (We had heard the woman's agony waiting for the delivery of the child.) Dr. Medina had to leave the side of Dr. Pratt to seek to deliver the baby, thus leaving the surgical team critically short of experienced help.

However, shortly thereafter it was obvious that something serious had gone wrong, which we could deduce from the activities of the medical staff. It had been a very difficult delivery. Later the doctors were to say, "If only we had had another physician," for she required a cesarean section. That was not possible with the tiny staff, given the fact that the operation upon Dr. Neufeld was well under way. In the end Dr. Pratt had to leave the operation upon Dr. Neufeld in the middle of the surgery, leaving two nurses to monitor his condition and report if there was any evidence of complications. It was a difficult decision but a decision and choice which the doctors had to make. However, every effort the doctors made for the survival of the mother and the little son proved futile. Both died. What a tragedy! I still remember a staff member wheeling out the bodies of the mother with the child, less visible, resting on the mother's abdomen under a sheet. It caused feelings of great anguish.

How I pray that many more of our physicians and surgeons would see it as their responsibility to minister sacrificially in service in these needy areas of the world. This is also true of nursing staff and other paraprofessionals so necessary in these situations. We learned later that the deceased mother had said she felt that she was going to die with this twelfth child. We could hardly imagine the distress of the family. The husband was now left with eleven children and no wife and mother to bring the children up to young adults. This was just symptomatic of the terrible pain that there has been down through the ages when a mother has died while her children are still very young.

In spite of the difficult situation, the doctors returned to complete the operation so necessary for the survival of Dr. Neufeld. This they did and did successfully, having to remove nearly two feet of the doctor's intestines. As we left, he was on the way to what proved to be a full recovery. We thank God that He protected one of His faithful, sacrificial servants.

"I Must Have My Quiver Full"

1971

IN the months leading up to the general Parliamentary elections in Jamaica early in 1972, my wife and I had become good friends with the Gallimore family. Dr. Neville Gallimore, a physician, had graduated with his undergraduate degree from Pacific Union College and had trained in the well-known medical school at Guadalajara, Mexico. At the age of 28, he had succeeded his father as the member of parliament for Southwestern St. Anne. This was a rural constituency where in some areas the people were illiterate or almost illiterate. Mr. Gallimore, senior, had first won the seat in the 1950s. He had been defeated at the next election, but from thereon either he or his son held that seat. It became known as the "Gallimore seat."

On the occasion of our weekend visit to Neville and his wife, Angela, we were told that on the Sunday they were visiting a part of the constituency in a remote area where the people almost exclusively voted for Gallimore. Indeed in the previous election of the 121 registered voters, 118 voted for Dr. Gallimore. The fact that three did not, made the people in that valley very angry. They sought to find out who the three were who had dared to vote the for the opposition candidate. They never did discover who these three were, and that was very providential, for they may well have done very serious bodily harm to them. Such is politics in Jamaica.

However, on this occasion, Dr. Gallimore told me that he did not need to give a long political speech, and he would like me to speak to the people. In the little valley, there was an independent church, and Dr. Gallimore arranged for me to speak at that church. Many of the people in that region were illiterate. Overall, at the time about nineteen percent of Jamaicans were illiterate and almost all of those were in remote rural parts, an example of which we visited that day. I had no idea what to expect as we reached the little, roughly constructed church. However, the church was packed. We wondered when the song service would close. For each song the leader of the church would recite a line and then, as slowly as it was imaginable, the people would sing that line, this being repeated until the hymn was completed. One hymn took over a quarter of an hour to complete with this process and commonly it took ten minutes because of the unbelievable slowness with which each line was sung. Eventually it was my responsibility to preach.

I very quickly realized that this was a Pentecostal group of people. I could say almost nothing with emphasis or strength before there were outrageous verbal responses from the congregation. I decided to use as passive and as unemotive words as I could in the hope that I could somehow dispel this kind of influence as I was speaking. Indeed, on the whole I succeeded except once in awhile there would be an emotional outburst. However, the people were not to be denied their determination for the meeting to have Pentecostal demonstrations. As we began to sing the closing hymn one woman shouted out, "Go up, Moses!" and then raced out of the church. We could hear her running up and down the road in front of the church repeating "Go up, Moses! Go up, Moses!" Then she came back into the church and started literally to dance on her knees. It must have been painful—knee dancing on the hard board floor of that church. Soon others were joining her, and not only were they dancing but they were shouting and calling out. It certainly was a bedlam of noise, and total confusion reigned. I noticed the two younger sons of the Gallimores were up on their feet laughing. Sadly this was great entertainment for them.

However, I was greatly grieved for I knew that this was not the spirit of Christ in the midst of these people. Indeed, not half an hour after the service ended, the woman who had first run out of the church was down by the village jukebox, which was spewing out wild reggae music, and she was now dancing to that music. It gave me no confidence that her first demonstration was led by the Holy Spirit. I believe both her dancing in the church and at the jukebox were equally inspired by the arch deceiver. It is customary with politicians when they visit an area, especially in the country, to make political speeches. They also provide, for the people a curried goat feast, free of charge. Politicians pay for the goats to be slaughtered, and then they have some of the local women prepare the feast. This took place again on this occasion. Of course, there were other things to eat besides curried goat and we were able to have a reasonable meal.

After the meal about 200 people, including children, gathered around a utility truck which Mr. Gallimore senior had driven to the meeting. He was there with his wife to support his son. Mrs. Gallimore, Sr., was quite a woman in her own right. For many years, she was a member of the council for the parish of Saint Anne, and she received a high honor from the government for her long years of public service. After the feast Mr. Gallimore senior extolled all the things he had done as member for that area, so much so that his wife whispered to him, "Tell them about what Neville has done." Then he launched into all the things that his son had accomplished and was doing and planned to do for the people in that area. One of the most important achievements which they accomplished for the people was to build a little water dam so that the people did not have to walk two miles up and down the hill to obtain their water. This was considered a tremendous blessing to the people, and they were very grateful for it.

After Mr. Gallimore senior, mother Gallimore made a short speech, and then Neville made also a short speech. Then Neville opened the opportunity for the people to speak out. All spoke in patois. By this time my wife could understand it well and I could understand the main meaning of this local ungrammatical language. One man cried out, naming the opponent who was to stand against Neville Gallimore in the 1972 elections, and saying (I am translating this into regular English), "We will eat his curried goat, but we will not vote for him." Many cries of expressions of love and devotion and dedication arose from the people. Perhaps the comment that most staggered my wife and me was from a woman. She had very few teeth left in her gums, but she certainly was an enthusiastic supporter of "the doctor." It was hard for my wife and I not to burst out laughing when she said, "Now we have the dam. We don't have to walk a long way to get water, and now I don't have to wash my hands in wee-wee." We noticed that not one person in the crowd showed any mirth at such a statement. Yet it certainly was a statement that made it hard to contain ourselves from a responsive laughter.

Then Dr. Gallimore introduced my wife and me and told them that what they really needed was not a political talk from him but a spiritual talk from me. They listened very attentively as I opened the gospel to them. Somehow outside the church there was not the same Pentecostal response. They seemed appreciative of the message which I preached to them from the back of the utility vehicle.

After I had preached, a man in his 30s approached me, asking whether he could speak privately with me. This I consented to do while other activities were taking place. He told me he had a great problem and he was a very poor man and he did not know what to do. I asked him what his problem was. He told me he already had five children and two more were soon to be born. While I did not really expect that he had a wife who was soon to have twins, nevertheless, I responded to him, "Is your wife soon to have twins?" The poor man hung his head and said, "No, Pastor, two women." I asked him how many women were responsible for the five children he had and the two which were soon to be born. Again he hung his head and said, "Three." I started to talk with him about being a moral and upright man, but before I could proceed very far he somehow thought that I was counseling him to use contraceptives. That was not in my mind. Around Jamaica are myriads of signs urging that contraceptives be used, but many Jamaicans do not believe in using contraception. Thus when this man thought I was suggesting contraception to him he said, "No, Pastor, I must have my quiver full." This is not an uncommon statement in Jamaica by men who have many children, often by multiple wives or mistresses. It seemed that one of the best known passages in all the Scripture was Psalm 127:4–5:

> As arrows are in the hand of a mighty man; so are children of the youth. Happy is the man that hath his

quiver full of them: they shall not be ashamed, but they shall speak with the enemies in the gate.

This man certainly knew that text and applied it to himself. His burden was not to stop having children but how to get more money to support them. I spoke to him very strongly about making a moral decision. I found that he was married to none of these women, and, like so many men in Jamaica, he was itinerating between them, staying with each one on a periodic basis. This is sadly a common practice in Jamaica, especially among the uneducated people. They give a little money to each one of these mistresses, never enough to be adequate, and these women keep bearing children to them. It is an extraordinarily difficult thing for them to break away from these practices, and the women are almost held in bondage through fear of consequences should they decide no longer to serve the immoral desires of such men. However, I pled with this man to become a true Christian and to marry but one wife and be loyal to her and to no one else. I know that would have been a difficult decision for him to make, but it was the only proper decision which he could make. When explaining his opposition to contraception, he said to me, "I know corn will not grow if it is boiled." Somehow he had the belief that if one used contraception it would destroy his manliness. Such are the false views of some of the uneducated people in Jamaica.

Blessed Experiences in Jamaica

1970–1972

LESS than two weeks after my wife and I had arrived in Jamaica, the ingathering campaign was in full swing. Every year students and staff from West Indies College fanned out over the island to ingather, usually with excellent results. Some of the staff had their special areas where they had ingathered for years in businesses, especially in the larger cities such as Kingston, Montego Bay, and Spanish Town. West Indies Union counted upon a large influx of funds from the college's ingathering efforts.

I agreed to take a group of students to the north coast of Jamaica, east from Montego Bay. The students with me were very anxious to go to the wealthy homes, where they believed they would receive large donations. However this proved to be a false hope. Most of these beautiful places on the north coast were owned by successful businessmen and industrialists, usually from Kingston, who occupied them for weekend retreats as well as vacations. Thus in most cases all the students found were maids who either had no money or very little money, and therefore the contributions were very little indeed.

Unfortunately, at West Indies College there was a great thrust to be very successful because special prizes and scholarships were given to students who did very well. Conferences usually gave scholarships not only for the students who collected the most overall, but they would also give a prize for the student from each of the thirteen parishes (counties) who collected the highest funds. I found this to be a very counterproductive process, and the next year when I was now president I determined to have this changed. I had found that there were many students who did not choose to participate in the ingathering campaign because, they said, "I'm not good enough to win the prize." The prize became the issue rather than the dedication to the Lord's work.

The next year I told the union lay activities (personal ministries) director that I would not permit any prizes to be offered. He was stirred up and said very nervously, "The students will not go out, and we will not reach our goal." I told him that if my plan failed then I would not be in a position to say "No" to prize-giving the following year. Of course I prayed to the Lord for the success of the solicitations without the incentives of prizes. The union lay activities director was shocked when in excess of 25 percent additional students participated when there were no prizes, and the amount collected was well in excess of the highest amount ever gathered in by the West Indies College students and staff. As a teacher, I discovered that offering extrinsic prizes or other motivation for those who do best in examinations or in a particular subject is almost always counterproductive. Students focus upon the prize and not upon doing all they can to be as successful as each is able. Perhaps four or five of the best students in the class are motivated in the hope that they will win the prize. However, there is a strange tendency for the other students to perform even more poorly than they otherwise would have if each student had been encouraged simply to do his or her best. Surely, doing the best for the Lord is the finest motivation to place before ourselves and others.

While ingathering on the north coast, I noticed two students walking toward me as I was waiting for other students to return. When they arrived, I asked them how much they had received from a very nice home 200 or so yards away. They indicated that they had not gone to that house because of "bad dogs" (savage dogs). I was too new in Jamaica at this time to understand that large dogs were trained to be ferocious as protection against theft or even murder, and those dogs remain the security for many people. I also found that there were two things of which Jamaicans were afraid—dogs and rain: dogs because of the potential to greatly injure, and rain because they believed if it rained on their heads they would catch the flu or a cold. Thus at the college, whenever it rained, you could guarantee that there were fewer students who would attend classes. However, not understanding the situation about dogs, I told the young people, "You must not take that position. Remember how God protected Daniel in the lions den." However, that did not seem to allay their fears. So I told them I would go and solicit that home.

I was not ready for what happened. When I reached the front gate of the home, five vicious German Shepherds jumped up on the gate, snarling, baring their teeth in the most menacing fashion. There were two dachshunds there also, but they were too small to be menacing. What was I to do? I had explained to these young people how they should have faced these dogs in the protection of the angels. I had no alternative but to go inside that fence with these vicious dogs snarling and snapping at me. But truly the angels did protect me. Not one of them attacked me. It was a miracle. I knocked on the door. Eventually a white-haired English lady came to the door. She was beside herself. Never in all the years that she had lived there had anyone passed through these dogs. It was as if somehow her security had been wholly destroyed. She was so frightened, all she could speak was, "What happened to the dogs?" I attempted to explain to her that God had protected me against them. However, she was so distraught that I could not explain to her my purpose. To this day, even though at the time I was only 36 years of age and strong, I doubt whether I would have been a match for five viciously trained German Shepherds. God is so good!

At the college I was deeply concerned about some of the student attitudes. Every year a new group of young people would come to the college who did not have the means to support themselves. They were put on full work-scholarship for a year to build up enough credit to start the following year. I soon discovered that the other students called them "grubs," a term that was considered to be quite derogative. Part of the reason for this was that most of these work-scholarship students did what was considered to be the most menial tasks of janitorial work and other physical work such as working on the farm. When I became president I issued an edict barring the use of the word "grubs" in relation to these work-scholarship students. The strange thing was that the students who had once been on work-scholarship seemed to delight just as strongly in calling the new work-scholarship students "grubs" as other students. It was as if "we endured it, so you have to endure it too." There was no evidence that they felt sympathetic, saying, "We did not like it and therefore we do not want you to have to go through what we went through."

The other students eschewed any kind of physical work. They wanted to work in the offices, to be assistants to the teachers—anything at all but to be part of the physical work. They saw physical work as degrading. No doubt this was a hangover from the colonial days when the British used indigenous Jamaicans to do all the physical work. Now that they were training to become professionals and leaders, they wanted nothing to do with what they considered to be the menial tasks of life.

So concerned was I about this that when I had many of the senior students, including the ministerial students, in my Christian Education class, I spent much time discussing the dignity of labor and how God had chosen useful manual labor to be part of the training for every youth, starting with Adam and Eve in the Garden of Eden. I read to them from the book *Education* where the servant of the Lord said that every parent trained his child in useful work in the Jewish economy. This did bring conviction to some of the ministerial men. I made an appeal for the senior ministerial men to swallow their pride, to follow the counsel of the Lord, and to ask for work on the farm or in other areas requiring physical activities.

I was very pleased when four of the finest students we had decided that they would follow the Lord. I told them that if they did, I believed that it would help other students to gain a new respect for this kind of work. The four students did an excellent work and were highly appreciated on the farm. However, to my dismay, I found that even though these respected students were willing to set an example, it did not cause a significant change in the attitude of the other students. Yet to this day I thank the Lord for the willingness of those young people who determined to follow the Word of God rather than follow the practices of Jamaican culture.

I remember how appreciative the students were when I would do something to help them. One of those acts for which the students showed great appreciation was in connection with the senior students of the college who were living across the road in "Siberia," a home which had been converted into a small dormitory for trusted male students, mainly more senior ministerial students. Those students had a relatively long walk up to the road, through the gate and then up to the college. They had mentioned to me what a help it would be to have a shortcut directly across the road to their dormitory. I decided that that would be helpful to them and thus I organized some of the staff and their student helpers to construct a path and steps directly down to the road in line with where "Siberia" was located. This more than halved the distance which the students had to walk to their college classes and other activities on the campus. In appreciation of this the students named the shortcut "The Standish Walk." However subsequently, I have learned from the Spirit of Prophecy that no building should be named after a fallible human being. I believe this principle would also apply to a walkway:

> In connection with every line of God's work in the earth today, the Name that is above every other name is to be honored. The gospel ministry, the publishing work, the medical missionary work, the educational work—all are of heavenly origin. . . . Let no line of work, no institution, bear a name that would divert honor from God to any man or any set of men. Let us remember that the beautiful temple which was erected for the honor of "the name of the Lord God of Israel," came to be known, through the apostasy of the builder, as "Solomon's temple." *Review and Herald*, January 11, 1906.

Many Jamaican students showed their great love and appreciation to us. Some became very close to us. Two who especially became close to us were Vickie Walters, who lived close to the college, and Jean Carey, who came from the Montego Bay area. Both now live in the United States, and we are in close contact with them still.

Another thing I appreciated about the students and graduates of West Indies College was their loyalty to what they called "the college on the hill." There was a dedication and a loyalty to that college which I have not witnessed in more sophisticated western world colleges. Students who had graduated ten, 30, even 40 years before, still had a great love for "their" college—the college on the hill.

West Indies College had been established in 1919 in a different location by Professor Cassius Boone Hughes, the same American who had established Avondale College in Australia in 1897. I found it interesting that I had the opportunity to serve in the two colleges which he established. Hughes was a man who undoubtedly enjoyed pioneering work. However, he did not live long after the establishment of West Indies College. I believe he died around 1925, though his wife lived to over 90 years of age into the 1950s.

Of course, more important than loyalty to a college is loyalty to God and to His truth, and I pray that the graduates of today will be as loyal as some of the earlier graduates of that institution were. Today, West Indies College has been elevated in status to North Caribbean University. However, it is important in the scheme of eternity to depend not upon its worldly recognition which has always been high, but upon its graduates who are faithful and earnest in their service for God.

More Jamaican Experiences

1970–1971

SHORTLY after my wife and I arrived in Jamaica, I attended a Student Ministerial Association meeting. These meetings were held on Friday evenings before the vesper program. Those who attended were the ministerial and Bible instructor students and occasionally others who might have had an interest. I especially desired to be at this meeting because the student president of this association had asked the treasurer of the West Indies Union, Elder Roy Williams, to speak on the topic "How to Get to the Top Quick." Elder Williams, a white Jamaican, was later to become Associate Secretary of the General Conference. Even excusing the poor English grammar, I was shocked by the topic, or more correctly by the motivation which led the Student Ministerial Association president to ask for a presentation on such a topic. However, the longer I served in Jamaica the more I realized how aggressively ambitious some of these ministerial students were. Unbeknown to him, I once overheard one of the ministerial students telling another student, "When I become an intern I will do anything which the president requires me to do. I will clean his shoes or whatever. But when *I* become president then I will expect the young men to do the same for me." The student was not a little embarrassed when he realized that I had overheard this conversation. I extolled him that God could not bless him with such motivation. It is interesting to note that he has not become a conference president. Indeed, to the best of my knowledge he did not become a prominent worker in Jamaica.

I was to develop a great respect for Elder Roy Williams. Elder Williams was a calm man and gave evidence of being a converted Christian. He also had a very fine wife. What was going to be the answer of this man was intriguing to me. Without any words of condemnation or reproach for the topic he had been assigned to present, his opening sentence was a beautiful response. Indeed, though he did continue to talk on, he could have stopped at that point. His opening words were, "Young men, you are at the top when you are where God wants you to be." Surely that is a statement which every Christian worker can take to heart. The servant of the Lord calls us to demonstrate that we are "ambitious for the Master's glory." (*Fundamentals of Christian Education*, p. 293) Parents should train their children with this thought and not with self-centered thoughts.

We had a very interesting experience in our home. We tried to help some of the poorer young people, and once a week we employed a young man to do some work and gardening around our house. He seemed a well behaved young man and we were happy that we could help him. However, in the summer of 1971, when we were on an extended itinerary to visit and preach in many of the island nations of the Caribbean, an incident occurred which was quite shocking to us when we realized what had happened while we were away. One Sabbath the young man, who was not a Seventh-day Adventist, had returned to our house. As they were looking down into the valley where our home was located, some of the young men who were outside the chapel in the break between Sabbath School and the Divine Service spotted the young man. In good Jamaican fashion, they believed he was probably attempting to rob our home, and an "army" of young men raced down to apprehend him. Of course, he was scared by these young men. They accused him of trying to break into our house to steal. Jamaicans are always very quick to act in situations like this. In the end the young man had to tell them the real reason he was there to avoid what consequences might have taken place. Unbeknown to us, in the woods adjacent to our home he had cleared out a patch, and there he was growing ganga (marijuana). Only when he took the young men to the spot and they could see the marijuana growing, did they believe him. Of course, he could have gone to jail for this. Eventually the students allowed him to go. However he never returned, and thus we never saw him again. We often wondered what the police would have done if the ganga had been discovered and we could not give an adequate explanation for it growing there. The ganga was destroyed by the college staff before we returned.

Once a year a large agricultural show (fair) was held in the Denbeigh show ground, in the parish of Clarendon between Mandeville, where the college is located, and Kingston, Jamaica's capital and largest city. My wife and I attended it for one day. The special guest at the ground was the then president of Sierra Leone from the west coast of Africa. This man with his entourage was sitting in a covered area. He seemed a very harsh individual. Later I was to discover he was quite ruthless. He had faced an attempted coup; however, one of the army officers who helped plan the coup decided not to participate in it and had warned the president. Yet he was executed along with the others who were planning to take part in the attempted coup.

During the day it began to rain, and there was very little cover in the show ground, so large numbers did their best to get under the covered podium where the president of Sierra Leone and his entourage were sitting. Among them were Cheryl and me. After a little while I felt something strange in the area of my hip pocket. I sensed someone was trying to snatch my wallet. I quickly turned around and there was a man with his boy. As soon as I looked at him he crouched down, making it very plain that he was the one seeking to remove my wallet. I quickly felt for my wallet. It was still there but what was missing was my comb. I suppose I had to be thankful that in his efforts he had picked my comb rather than my wallet. I could have called out that he was a thief, and many men would have rushed to hold him until the police came. I decided not to do so. I knew just how Jamaicans might treat such a one.

At the same show, we were leaving when we found a little boy wandering and crying for his parents. No one seemed to be taking much notice of him. So my wife and I took him and tried to find out from him where he had last seen his parents. We gathered it was inside the show grounds although he was outside. So we told the officials we were going back in to see whether we could find his parents. In the huge crowd we thought this was going to be very difficulty. However we did not want him wandering loosely around because great harm could come to him. Once again our prayers were wonderfully answered when, not long after we had returned inside, his distraught mother saw him and was so thankful to be reunited with the son just as the son was happy to be united with his mother. One always feels a little joy when he has the opportunity to assist in situations like this.

Demon Possession—Again

1971–1972

AT the beginning of the school year September 1971, a fifteen-year-old young lady had enrolled in West Indies Academy. She had come from Kingston, the capital, but we were not aware of her full background at the time. Faith Forrester was an attractive girl, acting much older than her fifteen years. Not long after her arrival, a week of prayer was conducted by Dr. Harold Bennett, the new dean of students who had recently arrived on the campus. During that week of prayer, Faith took a stand for the Lord. It was then, and only then, that we had any idea of her real background.

Well before fifteen, she had become a famous singer in Jamaica on radio and television. Of course she was singing the popular songs of the day, hardly the songs true Christians would sing. However, her situation was vastly worse than this. She had attended Queen's College. This was an elitist girl's high school in Kingston. At the age of twelve or thirteen she had been receiving money as a ganga (marijuana) runner. Significant quantities of marijuana were grown in the remote hills and mountains of Jamaica. Those involved in the ganga trade used young, innocent children to whom they paid a small reward to bring the ganga from the mountains to the cities. The ganga was brought in Hessian bags just like any other produce which was brought from the country to the fruit and vegetable markets of the towns and cities. The complicated system which protected the top men in the ganga trade made sure that the children could not provide evidence to the police of their identity.

The children delivered these bags to low level gang members, and then the bags were flown secretly at night across to the United States, usually to smaller airports in Florida.

Faith was working for a nineteen-year-old young man who was building a reputation as a reliable marijuana supplier to his contacts in the States. Though she was only twelve or thirteen at the time, Faith somehow became infatuated with this man and believed that she had fallen in love with him. However, on one of his trips to the United States he was shot dead, no doubt over some drug deal. Faith was devastated. She believed she loved this young man named Jim and was inconsolable. When some of the other girls at Queen's College asked her what was the cause of her distress, she told of the death of Jim. They immediately said that they could put her in touch with Jim, and this led her into spiritism. Later she revealed that most of the girls at Queen's College would not sit an examination without consulting their Ouija boards to know how well they would perform on the examinations. Thus when Faith came to West Indies College, these spiritualistic practices came with her. When she took her stand for Christ at the week of prayer, she brought out her spiritualistic material including the Ouija board, and they were publicly burned.

However, the week of prayer speaker made a very serious mistake. He decided to take Faith with him on his preaching appointments to give testimonies at the churches, sharing her background and her conversion. We have warnings from the servant of the Lord that it is dangerous to talk frequently about Satan's power in our past life, even as a testimony:

> There are Christians who think and speak altogether too much about the power of Satan. They think of their adversary, they pray about him, they talk about him, and he looms up greater and greater in their imagination. It is true that Satan is a powerful being; but, thank God, we have a mighty Saviour, who cast out the evil one from heaven. Satan is pleased when we magnify his power. Why not talk of Jesus? Why not magnify His power and His love? *The Desire of Ages*, p. 493

> Let us not talk of our weakness and inefficiency, but of Christ and His strength. When we talk of Satan's strength, the enemy fastens his power more firmly upon us. When we talk of the power of the Mighty One, the enemy is driven back. *Messages to Young People*, 105

However, the fall quarter went by well, and then came the year-end break during which Faith returned to her home in Kingston.

When she returned to academy for the second quarter it became quite obvious to many that something had happened to the experience which she had embraced after the dedication of her life to the Lord. I talked to the principal of the academy, Brother Colville Jones, and asked him to keep a close watch on Faith. This he said he would do. Two weeks into the quarter I had an urgent call from the academy principal. He asked whether I would come quickly to the basement of the academy where Faith was acting very strangely. I rushed out immediately, and Brother Jones had one or two other people there with him. Faith clearly was in a very strange mood. She was sitting defiantly, yet solemnly, with her back to the principal's desk. Suddenly her hand reached back and grabbed hold of the Bible the principal had on his desk and started to twist it. I then realized that we had another case of devil possession.

There was much prayer for her, and eventually, when she was willing to communicate, the week of prayer speaker asked her to surrender her life back to Jesus. She persistently responded, "Jim" in an aggressive tone of voice, a reference back to the man who had been her fascination before he was murdered during a drug deal. There seemed nothing which we could do at this point of time when suddenly she began to rattle off with uncanny accuracy a string of words that could only have come from Egyptology. Fortunately, Elder Nembhard, the chairman of the religion department, was there, and he had studied somewhat into Egyptian history in his courses in ancient religions. He was able to identify some of the names which flooded out of her mouth as Egyptian names. Yet later she was to tell us that she had never studied Egyptology. There is no doubt that this was a form of spiritism and that Faith was under the control of evil demons.

We decided that we could not keep Faith at the academy, but the college dean, Dr. Herman Douce, and his wife kindly volunteered to take her into their home to seek to help her. This they did for two or three weeks before suggesting to the principal to give her another opportunity. This was to lead to the greatest disruption which took place at West Indies College while I was president. It happened on prayer meeting night. The dean of men, Elder Oswald Rugless, and I were standing on the concrete parapet upon which the chapel was built, looking down toward the young men coming to prayer meeting. The song service had already begun, and the dean was encouraging the young men with suitable hand movements to keep moving quickly because the prayer meeting was soon to begin.

As we were talking we heard a scream the like of which I have never heard before or since. Immediately we turned on our heels and ran to the other side of the chapel from where the scream was coming. Even though we moved quickly scores of students were already there, having raced out of the chapel. I broke my way through the students and there on the concrete was an academy student, a sixteen-year-old young lady from New York by the name of Joan White. The screaming was so deafening that my wife who was just about to leave our home to attend the prayer meeting thought it was on our doorstep, even though our home was about 300 yards away.

Immediately above the turmoil I cried out, "Did anyone see what happened?" Two students said they had seen what had happened. I separated them immediately and asked them for a description of what they had seen. Both girls gave essentially the same report. Joan had been sitting in the chapel. She stood up, began to walk out, started to run and, when she was outside the chapel, she jumped in the air and dived head-first into the concrete. Yet there was not a sign of any injury whatsoever. My first reaction was "this is spiritism." That was soon to be confirmed. I asked a number of the strong young men to carry her down to the women's dormitory. This they did, but a whole entourage of students had flooded out of the chapel and there was no way to stop them from following.

Joan was carried down to a circular elevated curve at the roundabout at the end of the road, and there she sat, still screaming. Suddenly Faith appeared, sat down beside her and began to cry out, "Get away from her, get away from her." Later she told us she could see the spirits all around Joan. I barely had time to say to the young men, "Get Faith out of here" before she too started to scream, in unison with Joan. It was a situation I had never faced before and certainly hope I never face again. I then ordered the young men to carry the two girls upstairs to the girls' dormitory—one to one end of the dormitory and one to the other end. However this hardly helped. Periodically the screaming would start. One would begin and the other one would join in in unison. Then there would be silence for a while.

By this time hundreds of students had cluttered the young women's dormitory, both male and female. They were praying everywhere. The girl's chapel was packed; there were students up and down the steps praying; there were others in the foyer; and they were praying wherever they could find a place to pray. Eventually, many of the faculty who had come for prayer meeting were at the dormitory. In the end, nine ordained ministers were there praying earnestly for the deliverance of these two girls. But deliverance did not come.

After some time I told the ministers, "There is no point in praying. There is something that these two girls are hanging onto that belongs to Satan." I could not help but remember the statement in *Signs of the Times* concerning the two demoniacs in which Sister White said that Christ could read the inner desires of their heart even though they were speaking the words of Satan:

> The demoniacs of Gadara, in the place of prayer could utter only the words of Satan; but yet the heart's unspoken appeal was heard. No cry from a soul in need is unheeded. *Signs of the Times*, June 18, 1902

It was the desire in the heart of the demoniacs to express their plea for deliverance by Jesus but the spirits would not permit them. However the evil spirits could not stop Christ from delivering them. Keeping that experience in mind I said, "I fear that Faith and Joan have no such desires." I had remembered the experience which involved Vivienne, whom God had delivered when earnest prayer was offered for her. I believed that she did have a genuine desire to be delivered from spiritism as was noted in her life subsequent to that event. However it was different with these young ladies. Something was not right, but what to do about it, I did not know.

After several hours I still was in Faith's room with quite a number of faculty. She had been very abusive to Mrs. Lucille Walters, the registrar. But now she turned to me in a pleading voice, "Dr. Standish, I need to go to the toilet. You know I need to go to the toilet. Please let me go to the toilet." I was not convinced that she was genuine, but, of course, I could not be sure, so I said, "Wait a moment." I selected six strong young men and told them, "If Faith turns toward Joan's room you have to stop her." The toilet was to the left and Joan's room was far down on the right hand side. When Faith arose she seemed very drowsy. She slowly staggered to the door but once she reached the hall she was like a wild animal who had been cornered as she made superhuman efforts to break through the young men and it took all their strength and power to bring her back into the room and to her bed. The screaming broke out again.

It was now approaching midnight. We believed there was nothing more which we could do other than to phone one of the doctors in Mandeville and ask him to come to the college to pacify the girls with heavy sedatives. It was very difficult. There was a Seventh-day Adventist doctor in Mandeville but to our great disappointment he was away that night and so we were left with no other alternative but to call a non-Seventh-day Adventist doctor. The doctor must have wondered whether the young ladies' dormitory was a madhouse. The doctor dutifully gave both of the girls an injection of a heavy sedative. At last the screaming stopped.

About one o'clock in the morning, wearily I repaired to my home, but it was very difficult to sleep after the tension of such an evening. The students found it that way, too, and we decided to postpone the examinations, which were to commence the next day, because of the state of the students after this incident.

The next morning, accompanied by Dr. Douce, the academic dean, I visited Faith in her room. Already the wife of the dean of men, Sister Rugless, was with Faith. When I walked into the room I asked Faith how she was. I had discovered that, in spite of the heavy sedative administered by the doctor the night before, both girls were dreamily walking around the halls at four o'clock in the morning. Faith claimed that she felt better. With firmness of voice I asked, "Faith, what have you in this room that belongs to Satan?" She responded, "I've got nothing, Dr. Standish. You know I burned all I had during the week of prayer." "Faith, what have you got in your room?" She tried to convince me again, but by the fourth or fifth time, in the end she knew that I was not going to be convinced that she had nothing which belonged to Satan. She said, "Well, I'll get something for you." She took out two pieces of printed materials. One was a small digest size book called *Witches in Salem* dealing with the witches in Salem, Massachusetts, in the early days of the American Colonies. The second was a periodical—a genuine medical periodical from the United States. However it was very easy to know why she had it because the feature article advertised on the cover was "Devil Doctors in the United States." I took them from her and ripped them apart page by page and burned each page individually. I believed there was no way that I could risk even a particle of this satanic material remaining.

The girls rested for a day. On Thursday night I looked at my watch and turned to my wife and said, "Well, this is about the time the girls started to scream last night." I had barely got the words out of my mouth when we could hear this terrible screaming again. I wasted no time returning to the college. I asked the dean to call the doctor to come again and inject the girls with another heavy sedative. I telephoned Brother Jones, the academy principal, and said, "Tomorrow morning we are taking these girls to Kingston." He agreed. We decided that I would drive one of them and he would drive the other. The girls would be in the back seat and two strong young men would be beside each of these girls. We wanted no distraction that might lead to an accident as we drove to Kingston.

Early the next morning, still somewhat groggy from the injection, the girls were loaded into the back seat of the cars, and we drove them the hour and a half to two hours down to Andrews Memorial Hospital, our Seventh-day Adventist hospital in Kingston, Jamaica. The medical staff did not know what to do with them. They kept them for a while, but the screaming began again. So they put Faith into the custody of her mother and they called the mother of Joan in New York and told her that they were sending her home on the next plane. That they did. I have not heard anything of Joan since.

I did meet Faith once just before I left Jamaica. She was then seventeen years of age. She told me that she was married and then she said, "Dr. Standish, I don't have any problems anymore." Sadly I responded, "Faith, that is because you have given your life over to Satan." I knew she had gone back to singing the worldly songs. I again pled with her to surrender her life wholly to the Lord. Sadly, I have no knowledge or evidence that that took place. This was a sorrowful and difficult time for me and all the students and staff.

There was another aspect of the incident which alarmed me. It was the number of students who wavered in their confidence in the protection of the Lord. They were so fearful after this event. For example, one of the young ladies who had told what initially had happened, who was the head student monitor in the ladies' dormitory, told me she had locked her door that night, she was so afraid. I pointed out to her that demons could easily pass through the door. All she had to do was to pray for the protection of God. Even more alarming, many of our ministerial students were totally spooked. Most of the senior students, who were living in "Siberia," the house across the road, refused to put the lights out that night because they were so afraid. I called a special chapel assembly to talk with the student body and to explain that they had nothing to fear as long as their lives were fully submitted to the Lord; that the fear which they experienced indicated they did not have confidence and faith in the Lord that He could keep them from any kind of attack by the evil one. It was an opportunity also to instruct all the students that if they failed to surrender to the Lord, Satan was going to do everything to take control of their lives—even to the point of devil possession. It was a lesson taken very seriously by most of the students. It is a lesson which all of us must learn—that we have nothing to fear from Satan if Christ has full possession of our lives. Satan has no power whatsoever when Christ is the ruler of our minds.

Sports in Jamaica

1971

JAMAICANS love sports and are very competitive. This did not greatly surprise me, coming from Australia where the idolatry of sports is also very great. I was well familiar with the fact that there was a strong rivalry between Australia and the West Indies in the sport of cricket. There had been no development of systematic competitive sports at West Indies College since there was no proper athletic field; neither was there a gymnasium. However, on Saturday nights the students frequently entered into quite a sophisticated marching program which was greatly enjoyed by the majority of the students. Also, below the college was a flat area where the students, from time to time, played pick-up games of cricket and soccer, and there was a room in the academy where table tennis was commonly played. Having not taken a firm stand on the sports issue, I did not interfere with these activities and, indeed, from time to time, participated in them with the students, at least in cricket and table tennis. Of course the students were always delighted when I participated, especially because their president was young enough still to have retained considerable skills in both sports. There was especially a desire for me to play various students in table tennis—a sport at which I had excelled in Australia. It was a sport in which I was considerably superior to any of the students at the college. Naturally they wanted to play in the hope that one day they would defeat their president.

However, two events occurred while I was president of West Indies College which greatly disturbed me and helped me to solidify my own understanding of the danger of sports and how they are inimical to the gospel of the Lord. The rivalry, competition, self-exaltation, and bad blood that develops when the referee or umpire makes a mistake and other such negative consequences are hardly a part of the life of a true Christian.

The first incident occurred one afternoon. I was working in my office when I heard a tumultuous uproar. I wondered whether there was a riot on the campus, so boisterous was the tumult. I quickly exited my office and witnessed a huge crowd of young people outside the academy. It was a mixed group not only of students of the academy but also college students. Many of them had been in class, and when they heard the tumult they had raced outside, leaving the professors without students. I was anxious to discover what really had taken place, what had caused this stirring on the campus. It did not take long to find out. There had been a cricket match between the Jamaican National Team and the National Team of Trinidad and Tobago. I learned that there had been an extraordinarily close contest and that, right at the very end of the match, Jamaica had defeated Trinidad and Tobago. All the noise was a great rejoicing of the students that their National team had defeated the other team. What had taken place was a vivid repetition of what Moses and Joshua heard as they descended Mt. Sinai and witnessed the raucous idolatry of the children of Israel as they "rose up to play" (Exodus 32:6). I realized that such responses were inimical at a Christian college, and I sought to explain the serious nature of what had transpired to the students at the next chapel exercise. Of course, I had to take a stand myself.

The second incident was much more serious. Many of the West Indies College young men also loved to play soccer, and some of them were relatively gifted in that sport. Located not far from West Indies College, in Mandeville, was a teacher's college, a well-known and well-respected teacher-training institution. Of course, the young men at this college also loved to play soccer. One Saturday night, together with a number of other staff members, I began to hear some disturbing rumors that a team from West Indies College had secretly played a soccer match against the teacher's college that Sabbath afternoon. We could hardly believe that such a thing could have happened. Nevertheless we realized we had to investigate the rumor in an attempt to determine the validity of these allegations.

I called the Administrative Committee together and as we interviewed one student at a time, we began to realize that the soccer match had taken place and not only were there eleven young men playing soccer, a considerable number of other students were there cheering for the West Indies College team. We learned eventually that one of the West Indies College players had scored two spectacular goals which made the difference, and the West Indies College team had won five goals to three. One by one, the players were identified—that is, all but the last player. We were told by a number of the players that the West Indies College team had played with only ten men. Yet we were very skeptical. It took into the next day to discover that our skepticism was well founded. The eleventh player was a young man already under strict discipline for another unrelated breach of the rules of the college and the other players were seeking to protect him. We may never have found out about the match except for the excitement that their success had generated, for they were bragging of their success to other students. It was one of the darkest moments in my presidency at West Indies College. Among the young men were a number who we would have never suspected would violate the holy, sacred Sabbath day.

You can imagine just how deeply disturbed the whole of the administration was. This college had a good reputation from the Seventh-day Adventist believers for carefully choosing its students and for upholding the principles of Heaven. I believed that the events of that Sabbath afternoon would not stay within the confines of the college and that great discredit would come to the institution as a result of the spread of this sad situation. However, our deepest concern was the great grief such an event caused our Savior. Of course, the administration had to face questioning from the Union Committee. It did lead to a very serious time on the campus, as there were many more students involved as supporters of the college team.

I realized that there was a deep spiritual problem in the lives of some of our students. This led to a special meeting with the students which resulted in many students acknowledging, confessing and repenting of their grievous sin. As always, there had been a number of ringleaders, and they had talked a number of the players into playing. Nevertheless, that did not excuse these young men who should have had the spiritual integrity to stand against any violation of the sacred law of God.

The idolatry of sports, I fear, will keep myriads of Seventh-day Adventists out of God's kingdom. Some see sports as innocent and of little consequence to salvation. But that is not true. The servant of the Lord has made some stunning statements. Here is the divine counsel that she received from the Lord:

> In the night season I was a witness to the performance that was carried on on the school grounds. The students who engaged in the grotesque mimicry that was seen, acted out the mind of the enemy, some in a very unbecoming manner. A view of things was presented before me in which the students were playing games of tennis and cricket. Then I was given instruction regarding the character of these amusements. They were presented to me as a species of idolatry, like the idols of the nations.
>
> There were more than visible spectators on the ground. Satan and his angels were there, making impressions on human minds. Angels of God, who minister to those who shall be heirs of salvation, were also present, not to approve, but to disapprove. They were ashamed that such an exhibition should be given by the professed children of God. The forces of the enemy gained a decided victory, and God was dishonored. He who gave His life to refine, ennoble, and sanctify human beings was grieved at the performance. *Counsels to Parents, Teachers, and Students*, p. 350
>
> The world is full of excitement. Men act as though they had gone mad over low, cheap, unsatisfying things. How excited have I seen them over the result of a cricket match! I have seen the streets in Sydney densely crowded for blocks and, on inquiring what was the occasion of the

excitement, was told that some expert player of cricket had won the game. I felt disgusted. *Ibid.,* pp. 343–344

Some of the most popular amusements, such as football and boxing, have become schools of brutality. . . . Other athletic games, though not so brutalizing, are scarcely less objectionable because of the excess to which they are carried. They stimulate the love of pleasure and excitement, thus fostering a distaste for useful labor, a disposition to shun practical duties and responsibilities. . . . Thus the door is opened to dissipation and lawlessness, with their terrible results. *Education,* pp. 210–211

"Pastor! Pastor! Let Him Through!"

1972

I HAD had much forewarnings about the dangers in Jamaica during a national election. The first such election after my arrival in January 1970 took place more than two years later. Jamaicans take their politics very seriously. They are fervent supporters of whomever they believe to be the right candidate, and this sometimes leads to violence and death. Unfortunately this fervor not infrequently involves the churches, including the Seventh-day Adventist Church, which certainly was true at the 1972 elections.

As the elections approached, the atmosphere was electric. It was hard to find anyone, including a Seventh-day Adventist, who did not have a fervent belief in one party, whether it was the Jamaican Labor Party, the then ruling party, or the People's National Party, the party which was to unseat the sitting government at those elections. To describe the parties, I would say that the Jamaican Labor Party was a centrist party and the People's National Party was more to the left. Most older Seventh-day Adventists seemed to be supporters of the Jamaican Labor Party. Younger members appeared at that time to support the People's National Party.

The union president, Elder H.S. Walters, was a close friend of the Labor Prime Minister, Mr. Hugh Shearer. He would call into the Prime Minister's office every now and again and, after talking with the Prime Minister, he would not leave until he had prayed with him. While I was there Elder Walters was awarded, by the government, a high honor only awarded to the most distinguished citizens of Jamaica.

However, it was disappointing to note that some churches took their politics so seriously that it dominated the election of officers for the church. For example, one church in the parish of Clarendon of which I was aware had elected major officers all of whom supported one of the two major political parties. No one who was known to support the other party was placed in major office because a slight majority of the nominating committee favored the same party as those who were elected to office. However, at the next year's election, no doubt by very vigorous church politicking, the reverse was true. There was a slight majority of members who supported the other party, and every major officer was changed to elect those who supported the other party. So intertwined is the thinking of the people between their political allegiance and their religion that they often believe one or the other of the leaders or parties is ordained of God to lead the nation, and they believe it is their God-given duty to support that leader and his party and that it would be against God to vote for the other leader or to choose church officers who supported the other political leader.

A number of Seventh-day Adventists were quite prominent in politics. That also included a number of former West Indies College students, some of whom no longer walked with the Lord. One of the practicing Seventh-day Adventists who was prominent in the Labor Party was Dr. Neville Gallimore. At one stage Dr. Gallimore was chief assistant to the prime minister and held other portfolios in the Labor government, including Health and Education. We became good friends with the Gallimores, but we certainly had different views on Seventh-day Adventists in politics. Dr. Gallimore had taken the position that when Paul spoke of the gift of government that gave him a right to be in politics. We believe that text has nothing to do with politics but rather to leadership in God's Church. He was a relatively young member of the government when we first met him although he was to become one of the longest serving parliamentarians in the history of Jamaica. His father had held the seat before him and so for many years it proved to be a "Gallimore" seat.

However, because of the dangers from opposition supporters, the Gallimores had to keep German Shepherd dogs, which were trained to be fierce protectors to patrol the Gallimore property.

As elections approached, politicking became very intense. Dr. Gallimore would not move anywhere unless he had about 60 self-appointed body guards, men who would protect him under all circumstances. As one of his body guards said to me, "I would die for the Doctor," and I believe he meant that with all his heart. No doubt other politicians had the same loyal support of faithful protectors.

We received warnings that it was increasingly dangerous to drive on the roads as the election date approached. We were told that motor vehicles, bikes or even pedestrians would be stopped by a crowd, and the crowd had one question, "Which party?" If the respondent answered the party opposite to the one supported by the mob then they were in serious difficulties. Commonly they were shot, not usually dead. For example they would shout, "Where him want it?" meaning, Where are we going to shoot him? Often it was in the leg and, of course, this could cause life-long injury if the bullet shattered the bone.

Yet there were times we had to travel. One day, about a week before the elections, we faced one of these situations as we turned a bend in the road. Directly from the rum bar, where no doubt many of the participants had become at least partly intoxicated, were about 200 people blocking the road. I had to make a decision what to do. I immediately rolled down the window and called out with a laugh, "Please open the way and let me through." Providentially this happened within a mile of West Indies College. My wife and I had been part of a crusade in this very region in which quite a number accepted God's Truth and were baptized. We were well known in that area, and the people seemed to respect us greatly. When they saw who we were some of the crowd began shouting, "Pastor! Pastor! Let him through." A big gap in the human roadblock separated and with a wave we moved forward. How grateful we were to our Lord because we were able to continue our journey safely! We decided not to go out again until the elections were over.

Meanwhile I had a great predicament on my hands. Many of the students at the college could think of nothing else but the elections, and it was obvious that the most vocal of the students were strongly supporting the People's National Party (PNP), the one which was elected a few days later. I knew it would create a terrible distraction on the campus and unprecedented reactions. Already I had had to make things very clear to the students. For example, I discovered that one of the students had written to the opposition leader, Mr. Michael Manley, and informed him that "West Indies College is a PNP college." In chapel I made it very plain to the students that we were not a PNP college, neither were we a Jamaican Labor Party (JLP) college. We were a Christian college. However, of course, this declaration did not change the sentiments of the more politically active students. I was praying earnestly, looking with dread upon election day and especially election night as the results would become clearer as to which party had won. By this time I was almost certain from every poll and information that I read that there was to be a change in government, and I knew that would also create hysteria, if not great confusion in the country. But, God can be trusted, and He certainly came to the rescue.

The night before the elections, the young ladies in their worship had a wonderful revival meeting. The Holy Spirit came upon many of them, and some who had been weak or even resistant to a true Christian life surrendered their lives to the Lord. They were so on fire that they asked me whether at the men's worship the next night—election day night—they could bring to the young men the blessings which they had received the night before. Of course, I readily agreed. We knew this would not be just a regular length worship but a very extended worship, as the young ladies would appeal to the young men also to follow the call of Christ. I knew God had answered our prayers.

As we were in the meeting, which lasted three or four hours, I could see one or two of the students very edgy. Obviously their mind was upon the election results, not spiritual renewal. They dearly wanted to know what was happening. They wanted to know the election results. But the young ladies were saying, "There are far more important things than an election." The young men who were so fired up about the election had little alternative but to stay in the meeting, whether or not they were responding to Christ's call upon their lives. Indeed, there were some of the young men who were greatly moved and showed a very significant change in their lives as a result of this meeting.

However, about two hours into the meeting it was just too much for one of the ministerial students. He left the meeting, and a few minutes later we could hear him yelling for joy as obviously he had learned that the opposition party had won the elections. It was a sad situation when we consider the futility of man and the omnipotence of God. It is wise for us to avoid any political party affiliation and, indeed, we are counseled that we should not vote for political parties.

> It is a mistake for you to link your interests with any political party, to cast your vote with them or for them. *Fundamentals of Christian Education*, p. 478

Yes, we are concerned about what is happening in the world, and changes in governments can give us evidence of the times in which we live. By their policies and the laws which governments enact, they can provide either civil or religious liberty or they can greatly restrict freedom, enacting draconian laws. We cannot put our confidence in the governments of men, for this is inconsistent with our total dependence upon our God and our Savior.

The day after the elections, we thought it would be safe to drive down to purchase some groceries, for we had not been out for about a week. However, we were wrong, for the heightened excitement of the change was obvious. People were banging on our car and shouting. They called for us to put our arm out of the car windows and raise a closed fist. I refused to do that. That was the symbol of the incoming party. The outgoing party's symbol was the "V" for victory sign made with the fingers. I refused to make either sign. Somehow they did not do damage to the car as they did to some cars.

As we passed by places of business there were people sweeping, sweeping, sweeping, symbolizing that the Jamaica Labor Party had been swept out of power. Every change of government apparently leads to this symbolic act. Everywhere could be seen people wearing orange, the color of the People's National Party. I saw no one wearing green, the color of the defeated party. It probably would not have been safe to do so. It is staggering how much hope humans place upon results of a political election. It is as if their future and their quality of life depend upon who is elected. If there is going to be a major impact with the change of government, it will be rather in the lives of prominent people, wealthy people, businessmen, industrialists and the like, not in the lives of the common people. It rarely trickles down to the common people. If only there were such fervor and commitment to prepare for the return of Jesus, who will make the most dramatic change in the future lives of all who are saved, then this would be a worthy activity. We must never forget that our kingdom "is not of this world." (John 18:36) Our hope is for the heavenly home and ultimately the earth made new.

"I'll Pay You Back When I Sell the Crop"

1972

THE second half of 1970, soon after I had been elected president of West Indies College, I organized a small crusade assisted by a number of the West Indies College ministerial students. The crusade was held less than two miles from West Indies College, so it was easy to spread the word around the homes in the area advertising the meetings. Usually such meetings are advertised by word of mouth without any special written invitations, but we did have some advertisements printed. We had decided to run the crusade because of a contact we had made with a Seventh-day Adventist brother who lived in the area by the name of Brother Christopher.

Brother Christopher lived in a very small block home and was a dedicated Christian who was anxious to share the faith in which he believed so fervently with those in that area. There was no proper meeting hall in the area. Eventually, we were given the opportunity to speak in a shed which was open on three sides. The operating of a crusade in rural Jamaica was a very inexpensive proposition and very simple to organize. No doubt this is one reason why there are so many Seventh-day Adventists in Jamaica, one of the most concentrated Seventh-day Adventist communities in the world. Indeed, back in the early 1970s there were about 360 Seventh-day Adventists churches in Jamaica. When one considers that the island of Jamaica is 148 miles long and, at its widest point, 54 miles, you can understand that with this concentration of churches, most Jamaicans lived within walking distance of a Seventh-day Adventist church.

"I'll Pay You Back When I Sell the Crop"

As expected, quite a significant number of the people who lived in the area were attendees at the meetings. This was a highlight for the local people, who by their very nature seemed to be more religiously inclined than most people in more sophisticated countries in the world—or even more sophisticated areas of Jamaica.

Just before the crusade commenced, we were ready to present a Bible study in the home of Brother Christopher when we learned that Brother Christopher's son was visiting. Carlton Christopher, 21 years of age, had just completed his service in the Jamaican Army. He stayed for the Bible study and seemed to show interest, although it was obvious that not long before the study he had been to the rum bar, for rum could be smelled on his breath. However, he said that he wanted to study the Scriptures further. I was somewhat skeptical because often such men make promises that they do not fulfill. So I was surprised and very pleased that the next week he was back for the Bible study.

There were others at the Bible study, and yet it took me several months before I realized that one of the young women attending with a little boy was Carlton's wife and the boy his son. The family attended the crusade, and they did not miss a meeting. When eventually the time came after several months of the crusade to invite those who desired to prepare for baptism and entry into the Seventh-day Adventist Church, a significant number of those who had been attending responded, and among them was Carlton Christopher and his wife. It was a great thrill to be able to see them baptized by the pastor of the college Church, Elder Hilbert Nembhard. They became very enthusiastic and faithful attendees at church.

One morning, I responded to a knock on the door of my home, and Carlton was standing there. He asked me whether I could loan him seven dollars. At that time the Jamaican dollar was worth more than the U.S. dollar—one Jamaican dollar was worth $1.20 U.S. Almost daily we received people, usually strangers, begging for money for one reason or another. My wife and I decided we would do everything we could to help those who were in need. Somehow they felt that because we were white we were wealthy. Indeed, what they did not know was that my wife and I, in our combined salaries, received only the fifth largest combined salary of the families ministering at West Indies College. However, we did everything we could to help. It was not uncommon to have up to three different requests in a morning. We made a decision not to hand out money here and there, for we knew that would only bring people who were really not in a desperate need or who would be manufacturing reasons to ask for money when indeed they were planning to use the money for other purposes which were not always good—rum, for example. A common request was, "Please, I need milk for my baby." We would always tell the requester to come back in the afternoon and we would have milk to give to her. Sometimes we found that they were lying. For example, on one occasion a woman came pleading that she needed five dollars to take her very sick baby to the doctor. I decided not to give her five dollars. However, I took out my checkbook and wrote a check for five dollars. I asked her to which doctor she would be taking the baby. She named a doctor in Mandaville and I wrote a non-negotiable check to the doctor. It was never cashed. It was plain that her story was a fabrication.

Now here was Carlton, asking for seven dollars so that he could buy seed potato to plant and hopefully harvest the crop and sell at a significant profit. I knew this was an opportunity to test the spirituality, honesty and the dedication of this man. It is very difficult for poor people in Jamaica to fulfill promises such as he made to me, "When I harvest and sell the crop I will pay you back." I knew that if he was truly converted he would pay the money back. I was wonderfully gratified when several months later, again Carlton knocked at my door with seven dollars in his hand to repay me. I knew he was certainly a converted Christian. I did not accept the money. That was not my purpose in the first place. It was only to test his integrity and his honesty in the situation. He passed the test with flying colors. Most certainly he was a converted man with deep integrity and most trustworthy. I knew he could greatly use that seven dollars, for he was a poor man.

There was another great reward for me. I had left Jamaica in 1973 to minister in the United States. In 1979 I returned to Jamaica for a visit with my old colleagues and many other friends whom we had made in Jamaica. By this time a church had been built which had commenced with the converts from our crusade in 1970. When the people in the area knew I was back, of course they urged me to preach in their church, which now contained more than 70 baptized members. Can you imagine my thrill when I discovered that, now 30 years of age, Carlton Christopher was the lay leader of that church! He had proved himself to be a true Christian young man, and now he had been recognized as the one best suited to lead that congregation. I have not seen Carlton since then, but I have every confidence that he has remained a faithful servant of the Lord.

23
"Be Careful, He's an Ignorant Man"

1972

I HAD been ministering in Jamaica about two years when I was invited to speak at the Robin's Bay Church in the Parish of St. Mary in the north-central part of Jamaica. This was a sizeable church with many children and youth, as is usual for Jamaica. As I and the senior elder (an East Indian) were shaking hands at the end of the service, a sixteen-year-old young lady came out, and as I shook her hand the elder took her aside and told her to wait. When we had finished greeting all the folk from the church, the elder said to me, "I want to tell you the story of this young lady."

Her name was Valerie Wilson. I learned that she was studying at a public school and was scheduled to complete high school the summer of the next year. The previous year there had been an evangelistic crusade in the church, conducted by the East Jamaica Conference evangelist. Valerie attended the services and made her decision to follow the Lord and be baptized. However, when she informed her father of her plans to become a Seventh-day Adventist, he told her, "If you are baptized, I will come into the church and cut you to pieces." Such threats are never taken lightly in Jamaica.

She spoke to the evangelist who said that he would visit with her father in the hope that he could influence him from doing anything that would harm his daughter should she be baptized. However, some of the members warned the pastor, "Be careful, Evangelist, he is an ignorant man (a dangerous and violent man)." With due caution the evangelist

"Be Careful, He's an Ignorant Man"

visited the home of Valerie's parents. There he met Mr. Wilson, explained who he was and how Mr. Wilson's daughter had made a decision to accept Jesus and become part of the Seventh-day Adventist Church. Well the members had warned the pastor, for Mr. Wilson became belligerent and shouted at the evangelist, "If you baptize my daughter I will come in to your church and cut her to pieces."

When the evangelist talked with Valerie subsequently, he suggested to her that because of the father's reaction it might be wise for her not to be baptized at that point of time and to wait a little longer. However with great courage and determination, Valerie said, "No, Evangelist, I want to be baptized now."

The baptism was scheduled for a Sunday afternoon. There was not a little apprehension as the members gathered for the baptism, for many of them knew Mr. Wilson and knew that this was a very dangerous man who had threatened the life of his daughter. Among the candidates sitting at the front of the church was Valerie. As the song service was taking place, eventually the people could hear a man shouting in the distance, blaspheming and cursing as he was wending his way toward the church. They knew it had to be Mr. Wilson. As they soon found out, he had been to the rum bar to fortify himself so that he could carry out his threat.

Shortly he was in the foyer of the church, brandishing above his head a large machete which he brought to carry out his wicked threat. Then he staggered up the aisle of the church, terrifying the members as he swirled the machete around. When he reached the front of the church, he scanned the baptismal candidates looking for his daughter, and again he began shouting with cursing, "Where is she? I know she is here. I know she is going to be baptized." But somehow God had worked a miracle. The faith of this precious sixteen-year-old young lady was honored by God, and somehow he could not see his daughter. He opened the door to the back of the church, and the members could hear him turning over furniture, thinking that she may be hiding somewhere in the back room of the church. He found nobody. He came out again demanding to know where his daughter was and issuing another string of curses. Surely God saved Valerie's life. As the father staggered out, he could still be heard shouting until his voice faded into the distance. There certainly is a God in heaven who honors those who love Him and serve Him faithfully! Valerie had surely stood the test of loyalty to God.

However, that was far from the end of the story. Over a year later I returned to Australia on furlough where I was invited to present mission stories in a number of churches. I chose to speak about Valerie and mentioned the fact that she would be ready for college September of that year. In two churches quite separate from each other, people gave me $50 notes, saying they wanted to help Valerie enroll at West Indies College. I decided I should make a major appeal to see whether I could raise all the funds which were needed for Valerie to attend West Indies College for three years. By this time she had decided to train as a teacher, although when I first spoke to her she said she would either do teaching or nursing. The cost at the time to attend West Indies College was about 500 Jamaican dollars for the year. At that time the Australian dollar was about $1.48 to the U. S. dollar, so it was even stronger than the Jamaican dollar, which then was $1.20 against the U. S. dollar.

As I set about to raise $1,500 for her education, people were generous, and very quickly that amount was raised. However, I had forgotten Valerie's name, so I wrote to the East Jamaica Conference explaining the situation and the circumstances, and inquiring whether they would please identify the girl and the elder of the Robin's Bay Church to learn more details about her. This they did and I wrote to the elder telling him that I had raised these funds and that it was to provide her full tuition for three years at West Indies College.

I received a fine letter back from the elder in which he showed how providential was the donation of all her fees to attend college. In spite of the difficult home in which she lived, Valerie was a superior student in school with a good academic record. There were two Americans teaching at the school where she attended, and they took a special interest in Valerie and told her they were willing to pay her way through an American college. She was thrilled at this prospect and her father was very happy also. However, less than two weeks before she was to leave for the United States she discovered that there were many activities on Sabbath in which she would be expected to participate at this college.

Then and there she made her decision that she could not attend such a college and violate God's law. She had no alternative but to explain this decision to her father.

Once again he was determined to kill such a foolish daughter. She ran as fast as she could, with her father chasing her. He caught her down on the beach of Robin's Bay and there dragged her into the ocean and attempted to drown her. She later told me that she felt calm and resigned to dying, knowing that she had done what God had expected of her and that she had the assurance that the Lord would protect her if it was His will. However, at the point in which it seemed that she would drown a man appeared and pulled her father away so she could escape. She never did find out who that man was. Some of the church members believed it was an angel who rescued her. But whether angel or human, there is no question it was God's intervention, and she ran as fast as she could to the home of the church elder. There she stayed for several weeks until the father was reconciled to her decision and his anger had abated. It was just at this time that, not knowing any of this, I was raising funds for her to attend West Indies College. The elder and the church members were delighted, for they loved Valerie for what she was—a most courageous, dedicated young woman.

Indeed she did attend West Indies College and graduated as a teacher and taught in Seventh-day Adventist schools. Her decisions were a testimony to me of the courage we all must exercise when the great persecution comes upon God's people just prior to the close of human probation.

"That Will Be It For You"

1972

I HAD a number of opportunities to speak at Seventh-day Adventist academies around Jamaica of which there were quite a few. On one particular occasion I had been invited by the principal of the Port Maria High School in the parish of St. Mary's in north-central Jamaica to be the week of prayer speaker. I was delighted for the opportunity. This academy was a day academy with more than 400 students of which about 70 percent were non-Seventh-day Adventists. The week of prayer seemed to be evoking a good response from the students. I had some very encouraging talks with some earnest young people, and each afternoon I had a room assigned to me where any student or group of students could choose to come to talk with me. Quite a goodly number came—not only of Seventh-day Adventists, but also non-Seventh-day Adventists. Some of them inquired earnestly about the messages which I was presenting which inspired the young people to place their trust and confidence in Christ as their Redeemer.

However, on Wednesday afternoon, shortly after the close of school for the day, two strong seventeen-year-old young men strode into the room. Immediately I realized that these young men were not coming for counsel or for guidance for they had an altogether different agenda. I greeted them and asked their names. The response of the first was enough to tell me that I was facing a serious situation. His response was, "My slave owner's name was Williams." I tried not to react to this knowing that any untoward reaction would be foolish in these circum-

"That Will Be It For You"

stances. After all these young men were between me and the only exit door which was available to me. They quickly followed the assertion with a challenging attitude, "We've got a question for you. What color was the first man?" Having been in Jamaica long enough to know that there was a small minority of Jamaicans who had a fervent hatred for the white race, it was obvious that these two young men shared that hatred. Calmly I explained to these young men that the Bible gave us no answer concerning the skin color of Adam and Eve. However, we do know that clearly, genetically they were the parents of all the different races which are in the world today.

Angrily one of them retorted, "That's a lie. The first man was black." I asked, "How do you know that?" He responded, "Because the Bible says so." I was staggered that these young men would believe that there was such an answer in the Bible, and I was not a little intrigued as I asked them, "To what text are you referring?" They responded, "Out of darkness came light." As you can discern, this was a terrible stretch of the Scriptures. They proceeded with their increasing belligerence and revealed that they were members of the Black Muslim Organization, an organization of which very few Jamaicans were involved at that time. They had carried with them a brown paper bag, and as they continued to talk angrily, they pulled out a book that had been hidden in the bag. It was a book authored by Malcolm X. At that time in Jamaica the writings of Malcolm X were banned. They could have been taken into police custody for having such a book if they were discovered. They spent much time boasting the superiority of Islam to Christianity. By this time I was becoming alarmed. How would I be able to leave the room? There was no purpose in further dialogue. Then they provided the opportunity. They began to shout at me, "You white people don't love us, you keep us in ignorance." And then one threatened, "If you come back to speak those lies to us tomorrow, that will be it for you." I knew the danger of such a threat in Jamaica. This was a threat warning me that I could be killed if I did not follow their demands.

However, because they were shouting, a fellow student, a young lady, one of only a handful of students who had not left for their homes, had heard the threats and quickly reported to the principal, himself a young man who had graduated from West Indies College only two years before. He quickly came to the door of the room asking, "Are you ready to come home?" for I was staying with the principal in his home. Was I ready to come home? You can rest assured I was! The Lord had provided a way of escape. Of course, the principal was greatly alarmed at the incident and sought the details of what had taken place. I provided them for him. He, too, was deeply perplexed. He explained to me that he had no idea that he had any student in the school who espoused the teachings of the Black Muslims, nor did he have anyone whom he thought was antagonistic to white people. However, as he pointed out, it had probably been some years in the past since a white person had spoken at that academy. Therefore there was no way of foreseeing the circumstances that had arisen. When he heard of the threat he said to me, "Maybe it would be safer if you did not continue." He, like me, knew that often when Jamaicans make those kind of threats they will seek to carry them out. In some ways it was a difficult decision to know what to do.

Of course the thought flashed through my mind, "If something happens to me that would be the end of my ministry." However, the Scriptures are so plain that God can care for His faithful ones. Thus my response to the principal, Vernon Cato, was simply, "If I were to leave now, what kind of a Christian would the students believe me to be? I have been explaining to them how they can put their whole trust in the Lord. If I were to leave it would show that I could preach the truth but not live the truth." With that, it was decided that I would continue the series. In the home worships, both in the evening and in the following morning, we prayed earnestly for God's overruling and His protection.

However, I must confess some apprehension as we drove to the church, which was located next to the school where the week of prayer was being conducted. The church was not a large church and was quite inadequate to seat the more than 400 students and staff of the academy. Therefore, a large number of the students had to stand at the back of the church, in the foyer or around the walls of the church. This made the circumstances much more difficult. Naturally, when I took my place on the platform, I was scanning the faces to determine where these two young men were. But, try as I may, I could not locate them anywhere until moments before it was my time to begin to preach, and they appeared at the side door, a very difficult position for me to observe their activities. Obviously Principal Cato had been looking for them also, for soon after he appeared and stood by them for the duration of the meeting. God was so good. Nothing happened. Of course, from time to time for the rest of the week I saw these young men in passing. Whenever they saw me their faces were grim, but no attempt was made to harm me in any way.

The week of prayer ended on a high note with many young people responding to the call to surrender their all to Jesus. The Port Maria Church pastor continued studies with all those who responded to the call to prepare their lives to become part of the Seventh-day Adventist Church. I was thrilled to learn later that 54 young people were ultimately baptized as a result of the week of prayer. From this experience I learned much:

1. First and foremost, that we can trust the Lord to protect us no matter what circumstances we are in. His angels are more powerful than any human being, and God has promised that "A thousand shall fall at they side, and ten thousand at thy right hand; but it shall not come nigh thee." Psalm 91:7

2. Satan greatly fears the presentation of God's matchless claims upon the lives of human beings, especially young people. He seeks to stop or at least hinder, the work of God's servants. However, when we are witnessing for our Saviour we must be fearless.

3. I have often wondered, "What would have happened had I cancelled the week of prayer on Wednesday? How many of those young people would have had confidence in the presentations which I made? How many of them would not have accepted the Lord's call at that time?" Maybe never again would there have been an appropriate moment to bring the truth to them in such a pointed way.

Thus we must remember that precious souls are the issue in every decision which we make. Whether it be by precept or example, we must share the gospel with the purpose of leading men and women to the kingdom of salvation. I look forward with great anticipation to meeting those who have remained faithful from this baptismal group, in the kingdom of the Lord.

"You'll Love It Until the Bloodbath Comes"

1972

WHILE president of West Indies College in Jamaica I had a number of opportunities to preach in the Bahamas. The Bahamas is made up by quite a few islands. Of course, the most famous is New Providence where the largest concentration of Bahamians live. It is on this island that the well-known capital of Nassau is located. However, there are some islands much larger, such as Andross and Grand Bahama, the latter's major city being Freeport. On this particular itinerary I had appointments both in Nassau and Freeport. Generally speaking, the Bahamians are friendly people and many of them are quite fervent in their Christian commitment. However, the Bahamians are not as responsive to the everlasting gospel as are Jamaicans. Nevertheless, we have some large churches among these people.

On this occasion I preached in the largest church in Nassau, indeed the largest church anywhere in the Bahamas. After preaching, I shook hands beside the pastor of the church. As usual there were many children and youth who passed by. While shaking hands, four young men came out together. I shook hands with them, and immediately after they had passed by, the pastor made the comment, "I am so happy that those four young men were here today." I knew there had to be a reason for that comment because nothing like that was said about any of the other young people with whom I had shaken hands.

After we had completed greeting the attendees as they left, I asked the Pastor, "What was special about those four young men?" He then explained to me the sad story. Some years before, the church had decided that they would like to have some special recreation for the young people on Saturday nights and perhaps at other times. They had no fellowship hall for such an event; however, the church owned a parking lot across the road. Thus they decided on Saturday nights to construct a volleyball court where the young people could "enjoy innocent recreation." Yet, as is always the case with competitive sports, it is never innocent. Some of the readers of this book may believe this is an overstatement, but we must recall the statement of Sister White concerning games of cricket and tennis, which no doubt applies much more generally to other sports, for these were the sports which were being played at Avondale College in April 1900 about which she was commenting:

> A view of things was presented before me in which the students were playing games of tennis and cricket. Then I was given instruction regarding the character of these amusements. They were presented to me as a species of idolatry, like the idols of the nations. *Counsels to Parents, Teachers, and Students*, p. 350

There is no question that it is very easy to be captivated by this form of idolatry. We must recall that God did not provide sports for the Israelites, for their recreation was to be found in useful manual labor. Thus every Jewish child, male and female, learned some kind of trade or occupation. Indeed, any parent who did not train a child well in such activities was considered to be a delinquent parent. Thus it was not unique that Jesus was trained as a carpenter or that Paul was trained as a tentmaker. No matter what was their calling in life, every Jewish child was expected to be proficient in a trade.

In the Bahamas situation, a number of the young men of the church became expert in volleyball, and, as is often the case, they were anxious to develop their skills in a broader, more competitive situation. These four young men decided to join competitive teams where they could play regularly. They became outstanding volleyball players. At the time I was visiting, two of them had become members of the Bahamian National Team and the other two were top players just below that level. As the pastor said, "They come to church when they are not involved in a competition on Sabbath."

What a tragic situation this was! What a lesson we should learn from it. What we might consider innocent fun can lead to great spiritual declension. I have known of similar situations in Australia, Great Britain and the United States where young people have been encouraged in sports, and then we weep when they leave the church absolutely mesmerized by the idolatry of these activities. Many others who may not achieve such levels of performance may still become "sports-aholics" and, if not in participating, in watching and reading about sports. This was a tragic situation.

I was accompanied from Nassau to Freeport by the Secretary of the Bahamas Conference, Elder Neville Scavella. This was the second time I had visited Grand Bahama. The first time we had held services in a smaller hall-like church; however, in the intervening time the new Freeport Church had been built and so this time I was holding meetings in this very attractive, representative new church. A large congregation was present at the meeting that night, after which I was shaking hands at the door. As I had shaken the hand of the last man to leave, I noticed a young man slowly walking toward me from outside. He had a huge Afro hair style and was dressed entirely in black. I put my hand out to shake his hand but he refused. Then with menacing words he said, "You don't recognize me, do you?" and then with a sound of triumph he said, "I'm Josh Maise." Immediately I knew who he was.

This man was a young Jamaican, though we were in the Bahamas. Not long after I had become academic dean of West Indies College I heard about Josh Maise. He was a young man from Kingston who had applied to enroll at West Indies College as a student. There were reports that he possibly was not a suitable candidate for the college. Therefore he was invited to be interviewed personally at the college. Because at the time the then president, Elder Kenneth Vaz, was indisposed, I led the interview. He came dressed in a way that I knew could not be acceptable at West Indies College. His dress was flamboyant, his manner was arrogant, and very quickly I suspected him of being on drugs. Desiring to know what the Jamaican administrators felt, I suggested that the chairman of the religion department, Elder Hilbert Nembhard, spend some time separately with Josh. When I asked the evaluation of the staff, immediately Sister Lucille Walters, the registrar, said, "We can't take that boy. He is on drugs."

After a long discussion it was decided that when he returned from his discussion with Elder Nembhard we would delay any decision, asking him to visit with one of the pastors in Kingston every week and from those visits we would receive from the pastor a report which would determine whether there was any character changes which would give us confidence that he would be ready to be a student at West Indies College in the fall. However the response from the pastor was negative. Indeed he only visited the pastor once and it was plain that he had not changed his character or his lifestyle. Indeed, he did not contact us again concerning attending the college. His mother at the time was working in Nassau, Bahamas, and after a short time she realized that Josh was not in school. Alarmed, she flew back to Jamaica and visited us at the college. She dearly wanted her boy in school. We pointed out that now we were well beyond the date for students to enter the college for that term. We also shared with her the reasons why we did not believe he was ready to enter the college.

I had only seen him that once and so his reappearance two years later in Freeport was a surprise to me. I soon realized the reason why he had waited back and had walked from outside the church in a way which blocked my exit from the church. Everyone else was fellowshipping together outside, including Elder Scavella. I knew this would be a dangerous situation, having had significant experience with what Jamaicans called "ignorant" (dangerous) men. There was every evidence in the way he walked in a swaggering motion, with his thumbs tucked in the belt of the trousers, and in the words that he began to speak: "You are the white man that kept me out of West Indies College." He then continued, "I am now a student at [an American Seventh-day Adventist College]."

Then pointing to his big Afro he said, "You wouldn't allow me to wear that at West Indies College. But I can wear it at ——— College." I pointed out that each college had to decide the standards which it would require of students. Then he started shouting at me, "Why don't you go back to Australia? Or better still, South Africa? You'll love it there until the bloodbath comes." He was convinced that I had been the one who was responsible for his being rejected as a student at West Indies College. Yet there had not been one member of the administrative committee, all of whom were Jamaicans, who would consider him as a student. He was convinced that whites will be eliminated from the planet by the black races. This was so foolish, but apparently he believed it. I hasten to say that most Jamaicans or West Indians have no such racial hostilities. Yet here was an angry young man who was deeply racist in his sentiments and troubled in his life.

I had no idea what to do. However, I had long before come to the conclusion that when one is in a dangerous situation you neither show fear nor flight; either way you are likely to be attacked. All I could do was pray to the Lord for help, and He did provide the help. Soon Elder Scavella came back looking for me and asked whether I was ready to go. Of course, I was ready to go—and that quickly! Once again the Lord had rescued me from a tense situation.

There is a sad postscript to this story. A year or so later I was visiting this college where Josh was studying in the United States of America and I happened to see Josh walking on the campus. When he saw me he raised his fist in the black-power salute. Still later I conversed with the academic dean of this institution, and I asked him whether he knew Josh Maise. Indeed, he knew him. I asked how he was progressing at the college. The dean said, "He has had quite a number of problems." That certainly did not surprise me. Among those problems was that he had been found to be using street drugs. He was placed on probation. This confirmed our own convictions that he was on drugs when he had applied to West Indies College. I was quite surprised that he was not dismissed from that college when that was discovered. I do not know whether or not he continued to use drugs nor whether he graduated from that college.

Josh represents a sad spectacle of many young people around the world who have been brought up by Seventh-day Adventist parents but who have gone into the unprofitable ways of the world. I felt especially sad for his mother, who seemed to be a very sincere Seventh-day Adventist. We must all continue to pray for our young people and for the parents of our young people, for there are great struggles taking place in the education and spiritual training of our children and youth today.

"I Plan to Do Nothing"

1972

AS in every institution as leader, a president has to take some strong and not always popular stands. I found that my first term as president at West Indies College was not easy. Being much less experienced then only added to the difficulty of some of the decisions which I had to make. Every now and again I would have a deputation of students—almost always led by the ministerial students—seeking some changes in the standards upheld by West Indies College. Almost inevitably, in one way or another, they requested that one or other of God's standards be lowered. These were standards which were not simply West Indies College's standards, but they had been adopted by West Indies College because they were God's standards. There is no question that West Indian college students can put a lot of pressure upon leaders, and these young men were not exceptions. On a number of occasions I had to respond simply, "Young men, I will have to stand in the judgment for my stewardship of the leadership of this college. There is no way I can agree to change a standard which is mandated in the Bible or the Spirit of Prophecy." While these students did not become ugly or bitter because I rejected their request, nevertheless, they frequently left clearly unhappy with the decision that I had made. This is one of the prices that one pays for the responsibilities in leadership.

Every now and again significant issues arose. However, I had a fine group of administrators, all of whom were Jamaicans, who supported me very strongly in any of the God-given stances which I took. This helped to subdue any student dissatisfaction, for they could not discover any division among the leadership. I have always found that when there is serious student unrest, you can trace it to division among the staff. All that is needed is a couple, or even one, staff member who sympathizes with the students against a principle or a standard, and much harm is done. Almost inevitably the only one hurt is the student or students who have been encouraged by faculty who have a misguided sympathy for the cause of the students.

Toward the end of my leadership in Jamaica two new administrators were added to the staff—one of whom I had strongly opposed because I had received very negative reports regarding this man from Dr. William Murdoch, who was then the dean of the seminary at Andrews University. He strongly advised me not to bring him onto the faculty. However, under great pressure from the union president, the board had voted to bring him as a Bible teacher. The other man was also brought after completing a doctorate in the United States. He was very close to the union president. However I knew little about him when he was voted to become dean of students. Very quickly I found that the new dean of students sided with students on almost every cause. There was little doubt—and this was confirmed by the other administrators—that he had a negative attitude toward me and obviously he was not a little unhappy that the president of West Indies College was a foreigner.

I did not sense this negativism with most of the Jamaican leaders; indeed I found it just the opposite, yet there were one or two who had their reservation. For example, one of the West Indies Union administrators said to me, "Nothing you can say to me would convince me that Australia is not the most racist country in the world." And then he added an interesting comment, "We can play with you, but we cannot stay with you." He was referring to the fact that the West Indian cricket team often played the Australian cricket team in international matches. It was true at that time that what was known commonly as the "white Australia policy" was in vogue. This was the policy which denied citizenship to almost anyone who came from other than a Caucasian background. It was officially called the "selective immigration policy." That is why, at the conclusion of the Second World War, more than 95 percent of

Australians were of British and/or Irish descent. There were very few even from continental European descent, and, beside aboriginals and occasional Chinese or Indian, it was hard to meet anyone in Australia who was not Caucasian.

The dean of students had been a soldier in a Jamaican regiment sent to England during the Second World War and he had had a bad experience in England. This was at a time when very few blacks lived in England, and this had greatly affected his attitude toward Caucasian people. Apparently, when they saw the West Indian soldiers, some of the youngsters of England would call out in jest or sarcasm, "Where is your tail?"—an inference that they were more monkey than human. Naturally this was a very demeaning situation and greatly impacted upon the dean of students.

However, now the students had two champions who seemingly would support their cause. For example, my wife and I were in Kingston where I was preaching for a weekend. Before I left Kingston, I learned that there had been great unrest on the campus. It was with a heavy heart that I drove back on that Sunday afternoon to the college. Before I had reached the college I had received five warnings about the great unrest on the campus. When I arrived back it certainly proved to be no exaggeration. The atmosphere was such that it could have almost been cut with a knife. I had no alternative but to call a special meeting of all the students in the chapel together with the faculty. The incident resulted from a student concert which had been held on Saturday night. It was clear that the dean of students had not well monitored the program proposed by the students.

The incident which caused the uprising revolved around a play which was presented at the concert. From what I was told it dealt with marriage, and in many ways it was demeaning of the sanctity of the marriage bond. The academic dean, Dr. Herman Douce, who was in charge in my absence, stopped the play because he believed it was wholly unsuited at a Christian college. The incident was greatly exacerbated by the fact that this play was presented in patois rather than in English. Patois is an ungrammatical language which has a mixture of English, African and maybe some French. Much of the student revolt surrounded the fact that the students believed the play was stopped because it was presented in patois. After Jamaica's independence, there was a great effort to preserve patois, and the students felt that the dean was seeking to deprive them of their cultural heritage—which was nothing of the sort. However, they were greatly supported by the dean of students and the new Bible teacher.

I spoke strongly that night, explaining to the students I fully supported the decision of the academic dean to stop the play. This did not settle the issues. I was up until at least midnight dialoguing with students, some of whom were ready to understand, others who remained hostile. One of the interesting comments which was made to me was, "If you had made this decision we would have understood it. But we can't understand it from a Jamaican." They still had the false view that their play had been stopped because it was presented in patois rather than English, when indeed the whole issue was the demeaning of God's institution of marriage.

One of the strongest student vehicles of protest was the United Student Movement (USM). The USM was believed to be the way in which students could demand their rights from the faculty and administration. I have never been favorable to student associations on campus. I believe that staff and students should work together, not in opposition to each other, for the good of the institution and for the following of the counsel of God. However, when I became president I had inherited this long tradition at West Indies College. There were a number of issues at the time, but I have long since forgotten what the issue was on this occasion. In any case the USM believed they had a grievance which should be redressed by the administration. I was always willing to address such issues objectively. On this occasion, however, I believe the officers of the USM acted wholly inappropriately.

We were conducting an evening staff meeting in a room in the West Indies College Academy when the president of the USM, a man who on the whole was a fine young man, entered, gave me a note, and then exited. I stopped the staff meeting for a few moments, read the note and then carried on with the staff meeting. Indeed the note was an ultimatum that the USM would disband if by nine o'clock that night they did not receive a favorable response to their demands. I knew if I yielded to this approach, worse things would happen. I did not share the note with the faculty, but I continued with the agenda which had been set for the evening. Obviously there was considerable curiosity. Intuitively I knew that the USM had the support of these two new faculty members. After all, the dean of students was an advisor to the USM, and I was almost certain that he was well versed in what these demands were and probably was aware of the way in which they would be presented to me. I felt sure that the other new faculty member knew what the situation was also. It was possible that one or the other had told them to present it in the early part of the staff meeting, assuring, as they thought, that the matter would then be seriously addressed by the faculty and hopefully in the favor of the demands which were being made by the USM. While it was only natural that there would be some degree of curiosity among the staff as to what had been handed to me by the USM president, I expected the greatest reaction to come from the dean of students and the new Bible teacher. Eventually that is what happened.

After I had proceeded with the agenda for at least half an hour, the dean of students raised his hand and asked the question, "Mr. President (Jamaicans were always very formal in the way they addressed each other and especially were strong to address each other by titles), I wonder whether it would be possible for you to share with the faculty what was written in the note which was delivered to you by the president of the USM?" In my heart I knew the dean of students already knew what was in the note. However, it was his determined effort to get the issue on the floor of the staff meeting. Rather than deny the request I simply said, "Certainly," and then read the note and continued to proceed with the agenda without comment on the note.

Immediately the dean of students raised his hand again, "Mr. president, what do you propose to do about this?" I responded, "Nothing." The dean of students retorted, "But Mr. president, this is a serious matter which could cause great problems on our campus." By this time many of the other faculty began to join the dialogue. Overwhelmingly they supported my approach of doing nothing. They said that we will not support such high-handed tactics by the USM. Eventually the dean of students said, "Well, what is going to happen?" I responded simply, "As of nine o'clock tonight there will be no USM, for they have disbanded themselves by declaring that if we do not favorably review their demands they will disband." There were protests by the two men, "But we just can't do that. The USM is an important part of the heritage of West Indies College." However that wonderful staff supported me in the decision which I had made.

When the next morning, it dawned upon the officers of the USM and ultimately the student body that the USM no longer functioned, there was great consternation. There was much dissatisfaction, not so much with what we had done as a faculty but with what they believed was a foolish action by the United Student Movement committee. I did feel sorry for the student union president, for he received the brunt of the student resentment. He really was a fine young man. For the rest of my presidency, the United Student Movement did not function. Interestingly enough that was the most peaceful time I had with the student body. There was no organization to stir up or manufacture issues or problems which they claimed needed to be addressed. Of course, students came to me with suggestions or questions of concern, but we were able to solve those on a very simple level. I found most of the students at West Indies College to be very fine Christian young people who were a joy with whom to work.

An Anachronism of the Past

Grand Cayman, 1972

THE Cayman Islands are made up of three islands: Grand Cayman (where most of the population lives), which had a population of about 10,000 people when we visited there; Little Cayman, which has perhaps 2,000 people; and Cayman Brac, with several hundred inhabitants. The people of the Cayman Islands are dominantly light skinned people of mixed African and white heritage. It was a place where pirates frequented in the heyday of piracy in the Caribbean and it is obvious that they were significantly responsible for the mixed blood population of today.

We visited Cayman Islands in the interest of encouraging some of the young people to train for God's service at West Indies College. However, few showed a great interest. Generally speaking, life on Cayman was very comfortable, and, by Caribbean general standards, the living standards were high. Many of the men chose the sea as their occupation, joining commercial vessels which plied not only that area but all the regions of the world. By this time, it was already becoming a haven for banks—a place where the more well-to-do of various prosperous countries of the world would do their banking to avoid the high taxation of their home country. This commerce obviously increased the prosperity of this tiny nation.

We were always a little apprehensive of flying to Cayman Islands because of the small, older aircraft which were then in service. We avoided travelling on Cayman Airways at that time because they were flying just one plane—a very ancient DC 3. Indeed, on one occasion the plane had proceeded from Jamaica some distance before it had to return when one of its engines failed. Nevertheless, by the grace of God, we had no problems on our flights, and the equipment now being flown there is very much superior to that of the early 1970s.

In spite of the fact that Grand Cayman is a small island, it did have some very interesting aspects to it. I will never forget walking along the seashore with Cheryl as the sun was setting. The magnificent spectra as the sun settled behind the ocean was breathtaking. Also of interest is the turtle farm. It is a very big facility where large sea turtles are raised for human consumption. Turtles are also harvested from the sea for the same purpose. It is not an uncommon sight in Cayman to see turtles on their backs, often left in the blazing sun until they are to be used for turtle soup or some other claimed delicacy. I felt very sorry for them. Many people are aware that there is actually a place that is called "Hell" on Grand Cayman. Its name originates from the interesting rock formations which could be well used for movies dealing with what some believe planets of outer space might look like.

However, on our second visit to Cayman Islands we were there during the time of the Remembrance Day commemoration. Remembrance Day around the British Commonwealth nations is the day which commemorates the end of the Second World War. I had been alerted by the mission president that there was to be a special ceremony to be held at the town square. Thus Cheryl and I, with a good deal of curiosity, desired to see what kind of celebrations would take place in such a little island. We observed that everything was done with the greatest detail, ceremony, and protocol. It was a small group which was gathered around the cenotaph. There were a few Boy Scouts and Girl Guides, one of the larger Seventh-day Adventist Pathfinder clubs, some police and a few other law enforcement personnel, and the representatives from various churches and service organizations. However, the most important person arrived in a magnificent, shining, black limousine, from which he exited in his beautiful white uniform and large white safari helmet. This was Mr. Long, the then British Administrator for the Cayman Islands. He was the equivalent of a governor had the Cayman Islands been a much larger colony.

As I watched the ceremony and the protocol, I could not but help think that this was an anachronism of the past. I thought of the days when all around the British Empire such services, smaller or greater, would have taken place. During the service one of the policemen fainted, no doubt, from the inactivity and the heat. That added a little distraction to the otherwise dignified ceremony. The main address was given by the Seventh-day Adventist Mission president, Pastor Albert Lyle. I assumed that such responsibilities were rotated among the few religious organizations and churches on the island. The Administrator read his set speech. Prayer was given and the ceremony was completed.

I had the opportunity to speak briefly with the Administrator. He was a man who bore himself with the usual dignity associated with the administrative class of England, but he was quite friendly during our conversation. He, too, saw this as one of the dying aspects of what was once such a common event around the flag in all British colonies. I did learn later that he was not a popular Administrator of the Cayman Islands. Not long before this ceremony there had been some unrest on the island as workers were calling for better conditions and higher pay. Apparently Mr. Long felt that the workers were getting out of hand and perhaps conditions were reaching dangerous proportions. There were hostile statements against the British government which seemed to disturb the Administrator, and he asked the British to send a destroyer, which stood off the coast in case the riots reached danger point. This greatly offended the Cayman islanders who were enraged that the Administrator would bring in a British warship under such circumstances.

By the time we arrived there it was clear that many Cayman Islanders had not forgiven him for this action. Of course, our first reason for being in the Cayman Islands was to preach the everlasting gospel. We found there were earnest souls in the Cayman Islands who eagerly received the messages which were presented. I pray that many of these have continued to be strong in the Lord and faithfully prepared for His soon return.

The Great Deception

1972

THE *Review and Herald* (now *Adventist Review*) had reported in 1972 that more than 3,000 people had been baptized in Haiti in one day. Never had so many been baptized in one day up to this time in any country in the Inter-American Division. This report clearly stimulated the mind of the West Indies Union president. After all, at that time the West Indies Union had the largest number of baptized members in the seven unions that made up the Inter-American Division at that time, and each year it was the leading union in baptisms. This may seem surprising today when one considers the fact that at that time there was only one union in Mexico, and Mexico was a country with a vastly greater population than the West Indies Union. The latter consisted of three conferences in Jamaica, the Bahamas Conference, the Cayman Mission and the Turks and Caicos Mission. The number of Seventh-day Adventists in Mexico now far exceeds the numbers in Jamaica.

The West Indies Union president devised a plan which he laid before the members of the West Indies Union Conference committee. The plan called for a special day to be set aside in October of 1972 for the baptism of 7,000 people in a day. At this time never had 7,000 people been baptized in a year in Jamaica although more than 6,000 had been baptized in a single year. When the conference and mission presidents heard the plan of the union president, they were aghast. They quickly told the union president that it was absolutely impossible, that there was no way by which there would be 7,000 people ready for baptism in one day.

This they said was out of the question. Indeed, the time frame was such that there was only a few months for the pastors to prepare these 7,000 people for baptism. With the conference presidents, I agreed that there was no possibility of such an event taking place with 7,000 being fully prepared for baptism. However, the union president was not to be put aside. He believed that if they put their heart and soul into the project, the conference presidents could motivate the pastors, and the pastors could find the converts to be baptized in every part of Jamaica.

The union president pointed out that Elder Charles D. Brooks would be holding a major crusade in Montego Bay, and they would hold the baptisms until toward the end of this crusade. Eventually, the conference presidents surrendered to the plan of the union president. However, away from his earshot, the conference presidents kept insisting that this goal was impossible. Immediately Elder Robert Pierson, the General Conference president, was invited to be at the baptisms to represent the General Conference. The initial date which was set allowed for Elder Pierson to be present. However Elder Brooks insisted that he needed at least one more week before his first candidates would be ready for baptism. Thus toward the last moment, the baptisms were postponed from one Sunday to the next. Elder Pierson could not be there that Sunday because Annual Council, which that year was held in Mexico City, was conducted at a time which included that Sunday. Thus Elder Pierson asked the ministerial director of the General Conference, Elder Reggie Dower, to be his representative during the baptisms. There was much fanfare as the day approached. Convinced by the information the editors received, the *Review and Herald* carried a short article. It reported that about 7,000 people would be baptized in one day in Jamaica.

The president of the union sought to arrange for a helicopter to be hired to transport him with other VIPs from one major baptismal site to another baptismal site in the various parts of Jamaica where baptisms were to be held. This would transport the official party which included Elder Dower, the president himself, the secretary and treasurer of the union, and one or two others. It was not possible to hire a helicopter so it was necessary to hire a small plane. However, the plane did not have the same capability to land close to where the baptisms were taking place.

This slowed down the official party from moving from one baptismal site to the next.

Cheryl and I had decided to travel to Montego Bay where Elder Brooks would be conducting his major baptism. The baptism was to be held in the ocean, not uncommon in Jamaica. Keep in mind that a coral reef makes it much easier to baptize in the ocean because there are no waves close to the shore. When we arrived, there was a large crowd waiting, and we asked Elder Brooks how many he had ready for baptism. He told us that he had 216 candidates. This was a wonderful harvest from what had been an extraordinarily successful evangelistic crusade. However, it was not the kind of numbers which would give confidence that 7,000 would be baptized that day. Of course others not yet ready would be baptized later. As we were approaching the deadline before the baptism at Montego Bay, there was no sign of the official party. As Elder Brooks asked about the situation I told him there was no way that the official party could have visited seven baptisms, given the fact that each time there would be a significant drive from the airstrip to where the baptisms were held. I said I did not expect them to arrive until long after the Montego Bay baptism had been conducted. Elder Brooks said he would begin the baptism at the time indicated. However, not more than five minutes before the published starting time for the baptism, to my great surprise the union president, Elder Dower and the others arrived for the baptism. I later discovered that they had only been to two other baptisms, as they had time for no more. However they had passed over a number of places where baptisms were taking place and flew low to give their greetings, as it were, to those who were participating in the baptism and to those who were there to witness the baptism. The baptism went well at Montego Bay.

Of course, everyone was waiting excitedly to know the number who had been baptized throughout Jamaica for the day. This was also very much on the mind of Elder Dower. I spoke with the Union Secretary, Elder Melvin Nembhard, an older brother of the chairman of the religion department at West Indies College. He told me that a number of times Elder Dower asked whether they had any idea how many had been baptized. He said the union president's response was, "We will not know for several days because there are so many secret baptisms which will have taken place around Jamaica." As the union secretary said, "None of us know of any of these so-called secret baptisms." My response was, "My guess is that not more than 2,000 baptisms took place." The Union Secretary said, "Why don't you try about 750 baptisms?" I could not believe my ears. I said, "Are you saying there was only about 750 baptisms for the day?" He said, "That is my estimation." He proved not to be far out as the number was fewer than 800 baptisms for the day. Of course, that is a wonderful number of precious people, if fully converted, who were added to the Lord and to His kingdom. However, it paled into insignificance against the boasted 7,000 which had been predicted to be baptized in that one day.

We learned that at the Annual Council meetings taking place in Mexico City that day, Elder Pierson, as the day began to draw to a close, kept asking, "Is there any word from Jamaica?"—meaning, Do you have any report on how many were baptized today in Jamaica? He was anxious to hear the report and share it at the Annual Council. However, no such report came. The day passed, and no figures were reported to the brothers and sisters at the Annual Council. Neither, ultimately, was any report published in the *Review & Herald*. Further the report of the actual numbers who were baptized would have been a very disappointing figure compared with the predictions which had been made several weeks before in the *Review & Herald*. To my knowledge no report was published in any publication.

Just shortly after the baptisms, the quadrennial meetings of the Inter-American Division were also held in Mexico, south of Mexico City. I was a delegate to those meetings. The Inter-American Division consists of all of Mexico, Central America, Colombia, Venezuela, Guyana, Suriname, French Guiana, and all the islands of the Caribbean. Obviously, when the West Indies delegation arrived many of the other delegates were inquiring as to what had taken place and how many had been baptized on the special baptismal day. The Jamaicans in their inimical humor made a joke out of what in reality was a very serious situation. I overheard one pastor mimicking Elder Pierson as he was walking up and down the meal line. The pastor approached other delegates asking mockingly, "Any word from Jamaica? Any word from Jamaica?" Everyone understood what he meant.

Perhaps the boldest response was made from a pastor who served in the Jamaican capital city of Kingston. When he was asked by delegates from another Union whether 7,000 were baptized on this baptismal day, his response was, "The greatest deception since the Garden of Eden." Many of the West Indies Union delegates felt somewhat humiliated at the outcome of the situation. I was saddened by the unrealistic goal of the West Indies Union president and the levity which the situation generated among some Pastors.

At these meetings I was privately approached by the General Conference Secretary, Elder Clyde Franz, who was the General Conference representative at these meetings. Many years before, he had served as secretary of the then West Indies Union Mission when Elder Pierson was the president. Elder Franz asked me how many were really baptized. He knew it was much less than the 7,000 predicted but was shocked when I told him the actual figure. I told him he could confirm it with the West Indies Union Secretary.

The major gatherings of the Inter-American Division are characterized by spectacular and enthusiastic reports rendered by each of the unions. Usually a number of spokesmen would give reports on various aspects of the work including the departmental directors and the college president. As the union reports were given in alphabetical order, the West Indies Union was the last to report. Of course, all unions gave very enthusiastic reports and inspiring details of the progress in their union. They also presented their goals for the following year.

When it came finally for the West Indies Union report there was no shortage of great enthusiasm and optimistic predictions about baptisms and other facets of the work for the next year. I presented a short report of the four year progress at West Indies College. However, the most outrageous prediction was made by the Sabbath school director of the union. When asked how many baptisms it was expected would be generated by the Sabbath school classes around the Union, he responded, "We have 7,500 Sabbath school classes in the West Indies Union. Our goal is for every Sabbath School class to bring at least two souls for baptism and so I am predicting 15,000 baptisms next year from the Sabbath School classes." Of course, this was a ridiculous statement. The West Indies Union had yet to baptize 7,000 in the West Indies Union in one calendar year. That included baptisms from all forms of efforts including evangelism, lay ministries, and so on. When the elder came back to the West Indies group I whispered to him, "What you said was outrageous." His response to me was, "If the union president can make such foolish predictions, so can I." I felt quite grieved that there was such trivialization of what should have been a most sacred and solemn occasion. We must never use the work of God to be degraded to foolish levity.

"The Lord Gave, and the Lord Hath Taken Away"

1972

THE most tragic experience which took place while I was president at West Indies College occurred Christmas day, 1972. My wife and I had traveled to stay with friends for a few days over the Christmas period. They lived several miles inland from Montego Bay. On Sabbath, Christmas Eve, the Montego Bay Seventh-day Adventist Church had conducted a Christmas play in which some of the children of the church were participants. No one could have foreseen that two of them would be dead before midday Sunday.

On Christmas day my wife and I decided to drive to a quiet place to swim. On the way we stopped at the Mahabee home. The Mahabees were faithful Seventh-day Adventists of East Indian decent. They had three children. At this time their sons were eighteen and sixteen years old. They also had a daughter nine years of age. When we dropped by the Mahabee home we found only Mrs. Mahabee and her daughter at home. We had quite a long chat with her during which she told us that her husband, her two boys, and three West Indies College students (one being from Kingston) had gone swimming in Montego Bay. She explained that the students had been at the church the night before, and she inquired of them whether or not they were provided accommodations for the night. They said that they would try to sleep in the church hall. Mrs. Mahabee, being a very gracious, hospitable woman, said, "No, don't do that. You can stay at my home and sleep there." Which they did.

On Christmas day, the college students indicated that they would like to go swimming, and Mr. Mahabee said he would gladly take them and invited his two sons to go. His older boy did not desire to go, but Mrs. Mahabee said, "Look, you may as well go; you will only get in the way if you stay here." So both boys accompanied their father and the students to the beach to swim.

While we were talking to Mrs. Mahabee we had not the slightest inkling that during that conversation a terrible tragedy was occurring in the water off the north coast of Jamaica. We traveled on our way, driving to another location and spent time at an isolated beach. On our return we dropped by the Montego Bay Church. There were a number of people there, including young people, and they were all in a state of distress. They said that three young people had drowned. Immediately we thought of the group who had gone swimming with Mr. Mahabee. There were six in that group. It was confirmed that the drownings were from this group but, no one at the church knew who of the three had drowned. This cast a pall of despair over us and all others. We quickly learned where the tragedy had taken place and proceeded there with haste.

By the time we arrived divers were searching for bodies. It was only later that I learned the nature of this freak, tragic accident. It seems that all six were swimming and playing in waist deep water. Remember, Jamaica is surrounded by coral reefs, so there are no significant waves of any consequence between the reef and the beach. It was like swimming in a lake. Yet suddenly the older of the Mahabee boys cried out for help. One of the students from the college quickly swam toward him. However in quick succession the student from Kingston also cried for help and then the younger son of the Mahabees. Mr. Mahabee later told us that he was able to grasp hold of his younger son and stand him up again. His son turned to him and said, "Thank you, Daddy." However, in no time he disappeared again and drowned. I do not believe there has ever been a rational explanation how all three drowned in waist-deep water. None of the three survivors could explain it. The survivors were not attacked by a shark nor did they experience a freak undercurrent. In spite of living in an island country surrounded by water with some fine beaches especially on the north coast, Jamaicans are not known to be good swimmers, and many avoid the ocean.

The Kingston young man was the only Seventh-day Adventist in his family. He had come to study for the ministry in September. I had taught him in a class and had marked his final essay examination paper just before we left to visit the north coast.

Those who survived were Mr. Mahabee, a student from the Dominical Republic, and a student from the Bahamas. There was one thing certain—Mr. Mahabee loved his boys. Indeed he had driven my wife and me back to the college only a couple of months before, and he spent much time talking about the hopes which he had for his boys to train at West Indies College for the work of God. This tragedy was difficult to accept by the members of the large Montego Bay Church where the family attended, and also it brought a great cloud of sorrow over West Indies College.

All efforts to find the bodies that day failed, although ultimately all three bodies were found. The last one, the younger Mahabee boy whose body was somewhat mutilated by fish, washed up on the beach of a very fashionable five-star tourist hotel. Understandably, the management wanted the body removed as quickly as possible. I will never forget Mrs. Mahabee with the help of some others covering his body and placing it in the back of their pickup.

The night of the drownings my wife and I visited the Mahabee home. One can only imagine the anguish of the parents. Yet what I remember most clearly was Brother Mahabee, sitting on the piano stool and quoting the words of Job, "The Lord gave, and the Lord hath taken away; blessed be the name of the Lord." Job 1:21

Eventually, the dates were set for the funerals. The funeral in Montego Bay for the Mahabee boys was to take place one day before the funeral in Kingston for the Kingston student. What a contrast these two funerals proved to be. There was such hope, such faith, such trust in the Lord at the Mahabee funeral as the father spoke of his hope in the return of Jesus to reunite him with his sons. The nine year old daughter sang at the funeral. It truly was a testimony to the family's loyalty to God and their absolute confidence in Him.

At the funeral in Kingston, none of the young man's relatives were earnest Christians, and their despair and lack of hope and confidence in the Lord was very apparent. Pastor Nembhard, chairman of the religion department, had the service, and I had the life sketch of the young man. Both of us found it very challenging to continue because of the wailing, crying, and even screaming, of the relatives, some of whom rushed forward to put their arms around the coffin. We witnessed a tragic contrast from the hope of the Mahabees. At the graveside some of the same scenes were repeated. Of course, our hearts went out to these relatives. They had lost someone near and dear to them. Yet we did not know how to comfort them, for they had no trust in the resurrection and the soon coming of our Lord and Savior.

Yet the story did not end with the funeral. Several weeks after the tragedy, a significant number of young people came from Kingston to West Indies College—possibly a dozen or more. They were greatly distressed about the death of this young man. They had thought much about his drowning and had come to many speculative conclusions. They believed that the two surviving students had done nothing to help save the life of their friend. This was an absolutely false conclusion, but nothing I could say could convince them. They demanded to talk with the two young men.

When these young people came on the campus there was great apprehension among the students, and, in good Jamaican style, when these young people were talking with me in my office, large numbers of male students had gathered in the hallway outside my office, listening for any indication that there might be some harm done to me. While the atmosphere was tense, never was there any indication that they had any thought of doing bodily harm to me. However, they continued to demand that the surviving students come to answer their questions. Eventually I struck a deal with them. I said, "I will bring these students in on one condition, that I will ask them the questions you have raised. We will run through the whole sequence of the events which transpired before, during, and after the drownings. You will have to be quiet and listen, and then at the end you will be permitted to ask any questions you believe have not been answered."

When I left my office to ask the two young men to come into my office, there was even greater apprehension among the students. They feared for the safety of the two students, even for their lives. I assured them that I believed that it was safe to bring them into my office. The students reluctantly accepted my assurances, and the two young men came into the office. Painstakingly and meticulously, I questioned these young people step by step—why they were in Montego Bay, why they had gone swimming, how they had been taken there, where they swam, and what had happened at the time of the drownings.

The young men had been in the water about three-quarters of an hour when the drownings took place. They explained what they had tried to do to reach the ones crying out for help. However, they could not explain the drownings. They had themselves experienced nothing unusual in the water. Was it some strange undercurrent? Most local people thought that was unlikely. Were they being attacked by sharks? Sharks rarely come inside the reef, and there was no sign of serious shark bites on the feet or legs of those who drowned. I am convinced it is a mystery that will be unraveled only in the kingdom of heaven.

Only after we had spent an extended time together and had completed the thorough questioning and responses of the young survivors did this group from Kingston seem to calm down. I believe that they realized that these young men were not in some planned conspiracy to either drown their friend; neither had they done nothing to help rescue him. This tragic experience was very difficult for me to deal with as president, but always there was the sustaining grace of Christ.

Disagreements

1973

CHERYL and I left Jamaica in April 1973. It was a sad parting because we had made many wonderful friends in Jamaica, and in many ways we loved Jamaica in spite of the difficulties which we faced in our service there.

On the whole we found the students to be very loving and supportive, and that was true also of the staff. I still count some of those staff members as among the finest with whom I have ever worked anywhere in the world, and many of them were not only dedicated but very competent in the areas in which they were teaching.

Because I was an overseas appointment to West Indies College, I was entitled to furlough once every three years. However, events were to change that situation. My relationships with the union president were deteriorating for a number of reasons.

I believed that there were financial practices which were being perpetuated in the union office which were both immoral and illegal. For example, according to the books, the union president owed more than 15,000 Jamaican dollars to the union, a very substantial amount. It had appeared on every monthly statement, and then I noticed its omission from the October statement. I protested, challenging the treasurer of the union, telling him it was totally dishonest. His retort was, "What do you mean by it being dishonest?" "I mean that which would put a man behind bars if he was found guilty of such activities in a court of law." It was left out of the October statement because, in November, the year-end meetings of the Union would be held, and at those meetings there would be a representative, usually a vice-president, of the General Conference and an officer from the Inter-American Division, and it was not desired that any embarrassing questions be raised.

There were many other questionable financial practices. One of many which hit me hard as president of the college revolved around an additional US$20,000 appropriation which was made by the Inter-American Division to help us complete the young men's dormitory. This amount was considered sufficient to complete the dormitory, and we were rejoicing greatly in the Lord. Yet when after five weeks we had not received the money from the Division, I asked the treasurer to call the Division and find out what was happening, for we needed the money urgently. I was surprised to learn that they had sent it immediately to the union president, who was also, of course, by office, the board chairman of the college. I immediately asked the treasurer to find out from the union president what had happened to the money. Apparently the president became very aggressive and told them he would not trust those of us in leadership "on the hill" and that he was handling the money himself. We discovered he had deposited it in his own personal bank account. It is true, he chose contractors to finish the building, and he paid them. However, to this day I do not believe anyone knows whether or not all that money was used appropriately, for it had been placed in his personal banking account—something wholly illegal.

There were other incidents where he had borrowed money both from Seventh-day Adventists and non-Seventh-day Adventists. I had two shocked students talk to me after they had been ingathering in Spanish Town. Both told me that they had solicited a business man for the Ingathering campaign. With considerable bitterness the man told them that he would give nothing to the campaign because only three years before "your leader" "borrowed $3,000 from me for two weeks, and he has not paid a cent back."

On another occasion an ingatherer in Montego Bay was turned down by a business man who had always given a sizeable donation. He said, "This year I am not giving anything. I see your leader flying around by private plane. If he can afford to fly by private plane, he doesn't need my money."

On one occasion, we were in a college board meeting when suddenly, about mid-afternoon, the president said he was leaving and told the secretary to conduct the rest of the items on the agenda, none of which were of any great substance. Minutes later, out the window of the committee room, we could see him boarding a light aircraft to be transported to Sangster International Airport in Montego Bay just in time to catch a flight to the United States.

On three occasions during my presidency, he had sought to bribe me in different ways. The first time, he asked me to come with him to the chapel. From the parapet at the back of the chapel we could look over the valley. The union had purchased a sizeable tract of land and divided it into more than 40 building blocks. The president turned to me with the words, "Doctor, choose whichever block you would like, and build your dream home." I laughed and said, "I'm waiting until I get to the new earth to build my dream home." I continued, "In any case, I don't have the money to buy a block or build a home upon it." His response was, "Don't worry about that. We will help you." Later I was to learn that every block had been reserved for one of the Jamaican workers. However, I had no doubt that had I succumbed to the union president's offer he would have allowed me to take a block which had been reserved for someone else. This was, of course, something I would never have tolerated.

The second attempt to bribe occurred after we had had a serious disagreement on issues of honesty. He told me, "Doctor, you are driving an old car. You deserve a much better car. We will buy a car and have it imported for the college but you can use it. Then we will not have to pay the 70 percent import tax." I told him that would be dishonest because it would really be purchased for me and not for the college, and I would not agree to receiving a vehicle under those circumstances.

The third time was after we had had a very serious matter of difference. This time the president said to me, "Doctor, we can still work together. I can help you and you can help me. If you work with me I will make sure that one day you will be in the education department of the General Conference." My response was simple, "Elder, if the Lord wants me in the General Conference, that is fine. But that may not be

His plan for me, and if not, I do not want anyone pushing for me to be in the General Conference." As subsequent history has proven, the Lord had other work for me rather than to be in the General Conference education department. I am so thankful to the Lord for His guidance in my life.

Toward the end of my ministry in Jamaica, I wrote an earnest letter to the president of the Inter-American Division outlining my burden for the many dishonest practices which were taking place in the Union. Not only were they practices inconsistent with the sensible guidelines set out in the Union policies, but they were practices of a serious nature. The division president did not respond. Rather he gave that responsibility to the treasurer of the division, who reminded me in his reply that I had been elected to lead the college, and I should keep myself out of the affairs of the union. I responded, pointing out that I was a member of the union committee, and therefore I had a God-given responsibility to be concerned that proper financial practices be carried out in the union. However, since the Treasurer had limited me to my responsibility as leader of the college, I would outline to him areas of financial irregularities and suspected dishonesty which affected the operation of the college. I then outlined 25 areas which came within this category. I finished the letter by saying they would hear no more from me. I was leaving it in their hands. It would be up to the division to decide how to handle the situation and decide what was appropriate action, but I prayed that they would realize that the decisions they made would have implications in the upcoming judgment by the Lord. Not unexpectedly, I received no further response from the Division.

It was a sad situation because in many ways I was very fond of the union president. He was such a talented man and a giant in the society of Jamaica. There was no question, no other president before or since has been so well known among the population of Jamaica and the leadership of that nation.

Leaving

1973

THE basis for leaving Jamaica arose out of the union constituency meeting, October 1972, just two and three-quarter years after we had arrived in Jamaica. As president of West Indies College, I was chosen as one of the eight from the college to serve as a delegate to that constituency meeting. I have been to some very tense constituency meetings in my life, but none came close in intensity to this one. Jamaicans by their very nature tend to be political in their approaches to such events. Long before the elections many of the constituents were very active seeking support for or against the incumbent union president. A strong wave of sentiment was against the reelection of the union president. West Indians, being very open, tended to make it plain for whom they were planning to vote. It was my evaluation that almost certainly the numbers were in favor of a change of leadership. While I did not express it to others, that was my conviction also.

As the date approached it was obvious that many delegates and nondelegates were consumed with the upcoming election. Thus when the meeting convened on the first evening, tensions were very high, excitability was strong. After the division president had made a devotional presentation, the various conferences, missions, and institutions were asked to choose their members for the selection committee which would ultimately choose a nominating committee. Both West Indies College and Andrews Memorial Hospital were responsible for electing one member each to the selection committee. Two of the Jamaican Conferences had to choose five members and one conference four members; the Bahamas Conference chose two members; and the Turks and Caicos Mission and the Cayman Mission one member each, thus providing a selection committee of 20 members.

However, there was great confusion after each delegation secretary had presented the names of those to serve on the selection committee. One of the pastors from the Central Jamaica Conference stood up and protested the five to serve on the selection committee from his Conference. He said the president of their conference had chosen the five delegates to serve on the selection committee, but the delegates had had no opportunity to vote upon the names. The division president ruled that everything had to be done decently and in order. He ordered the 36 delegates from the Central Jamaica Conference to reconvene and by secret ballot to choose their five to serve on the selection committee. There was much hubbub among the other delegates over this very serious turn of events.

Eventually, the secretary who had been chosen to represent the Central Jamaica delegation proceeded up the steps to the platform and with great pomposity addressed the Division president, saying that he now had the decision of the 36 delegates of the Central Jamaica Conference which had been voted by secret ballot. He then proceeded to name the same five delegates who had been read out before when it was claimed that they had been chosen by the president. There was not a person among the delegation who did not recognize that these delegates had been chosen because they were determined to vote against the reelection of the incumbent union president.

When the Central Jamaica Conference delegates initially met, one of the delegates had moved and it was seconded and voted that the delegates would give the president the right to choose whichever names he desired to serve on the selection committee. While it had not been done in the normally regular way, nevertheless, what had happened was legitimate, as was confirmed by the secret ballot. As a final act, almost in defiance, the spokesman for the Central Jamaica Conference said, "And Mr. President," addressing the Division president, "I have much pleasure in declaring that these delegates have been chosen to serve on the selection committee by a vote of 33 to 3." This told the rest of the delegates that only three out of the 36 delegates of the Central Jamaica Conference were desirous of seeing the union president reelected. This in spite of the fact that the union president was the immediate past president of the Central Jamaica Conference.

The division president then said, "It is now very late in the night. We will not ask the selection committee to meet now, but they will convene to meet early tomorrow morning." The excited chit chat when the meeting was dispersed that night showed both the expectations and anxiety of many of the delegates. I heard words such as, "We've got him this time," meaning that the delegate believed that the selection committee was strongly opposed to the reelection of the incumbent union president. Others said, "I don't know how he can get out of it, but he always seems to be able to get out of these situations somehow, some way."

There were other anxieties expressed by those who wanted a change of union presidents. For example, the acting treasurer of the Cayman Island Mission, a lady, had been chosen to represent that mission on the selection committee. There had been much lobbying of her long before the elections took place, and she had assured some of the lobbyists that she believed there should be a change in the union presidency. However, when, after she had been chosen for the selection committee, one of the same men approached her to urge her to vote for change she told him, "This is a very serious matter. I will have to pray about it." That same inquirer told others, "She's gone, she is praying about it." Meaning that he suspected she had changed to support the incumbent president, as proved to be the case.

We had had a very interesting situation when the college conclaved to choose one from its eight delegates to be a member of the selection committee. Out of the eight college delegates, five were Jamaicans and three of us were non-Jamaicans. Beside myself, there was Professor Wong, from Hong Kong, the head of the Science Department, and Dr. Andrews, an African-American history teacher. Intuitively I knew how the Jamaican delegates would vote—four were certainly against the reelection of Elder Walters. Only one would vote in favor of him—the college dean of students, who had been sponsored for his doctorate to

Michigan State University and had written his thesis on the evangelistic power of the union president. I had no idea how the other two delegates would vote, for we had never discussed the issue and they had not spoken to me about their personal convictions.

Some of the Jamaicans from the college delegation were determined that the dean of men, Elder Oswald Rugless, would be chosen to serve on the selection committee. He was a strong advocate for the change. Elder Rugless was a man of great moral strength and principle, and therefore he believed that there had to be a change. However, after he was chosen he said he would rather be chosen to the nominating committee so that he could make his vote count. Thus the Business Manager, Elder Aston Davis, was chosen to represent the college. Some of the other men told him, "Now make sure that Elder Rugless is voted to serve on the nominating committee." Elder Davis assured the men that that was what he would do. It was an atmosphere quite foreign to me and one to which I could not relate. Even though I believed the time had come for a change in the union presidency, I believed it should be done on our knees with prayer asking the Lord for guidance and strength.

The next day the selection committee met under the chairmanship of the division president. What happened thereafter I believe brought terrible discredit upon the work of God. I believe those on both sides of the issue were culpable in putting human devisings rather than consecrated decisions into effect. As the selection committee members reported later, it was a very serious situation. The division president told the committee that everything had to "be done decently and in order." Therefore when a nomination was to be made the first one on his feet would be chosen to make the nomination. But before that would take place they had to decide who would be automatically on the committee. Immediately the division president stated that it was necessary to have all four conference presidents, three in Jamaica and the Bahamas president, on the nominating committee. This was voted. There were those who said, "Also the college president should be on." The division president vetoed that, and indeed I was thankful because I did not desire to be in the middle of what was taking place. However, only one of the conference presidents was a certain supporter of the union president—the

Bahamas Conference president. The president of the Central Jamaica Conference was strongly opposed to the reelection of the West Indies Union president. But how would the presidents of the East and West Jamaica Conferences vote? In this part of the world there seems to be an unwritten practice that you helped me be reelected and I will help you. This gave the incumbent union president the belief that both the West and the East Jamaican presidents would vote in his favor, for earlier he had supported their successful reelection bids. Yet it was also known that they had lost confidence in the union president's leadership.

However in the end it did not work this way. While these two presidents did not vote for the reelection of the union president, neither did they vote against him. They both abstained, obviously not favorable to his reelection but nevertheless not willing to vote against him. So in the end that had not helped the reelection of the union president, but neither had it hurt his reelection because these two men abstained.

Then followed the election of the other fourteen members of the nominating committee. The interesting thing was that all eight of the members of the selection committee who were considered strong supporters of the incumbent union president were able to make a nomination. Only six of the twelve who were opposed to the reelection had the opportunity to make a nomination. The division president somehow had claimed to adjudge the supporters of the union president as first on their feet. As one would understand when two people are jumping together it is very difficult to decide which one actually was on his feet first. This immediately gave the advantage to the pro-union president selection committee member. No doubt, the division president felt he must help the union president, for the union president had been the "campaign manager" at the 1970 General Conference Session, which led to the election of the division president.

There was one other ploy that was used. The Turks and Caicos Mission was tiny, consisting of only 54 church members. As the Turks and Caicos Mission president could not be placed on the nominating committee because he himself was elected at the Union session, it being a Mission (as was also the case for the Cayman Island Mission), there was only one other delegate who could be put on the nominating committee. He was the layman who was serving also on the selection committee. Already the union president had spent much time to make sure this man would support his reelection. Thus those favoring the reelection of the union president were told not to nominate this man, forcing one of the six who believed there should be a change in leadership to nominate him. That, of course, made it more certain that the union president would be reelected.

Many things came to light after the session. We learned that a small group of close confidants of the union president had stayed up until three o'clock in the morning, strategizing how to turn a selection committee which was opposed to the reelection of the incumbent into a nominating committee which would vote his reelection. This was achieved.

It was amazing how easily some of the delegates were "bought." For example, it was discovered later that the woman who was the acting treasurer of the Cayman Island Mission had been approached by the union president. He had told her that if he were reelected it would be his desire for her to become the permanent treasurer of the mission. That apparently purchased her vote.

The pastor who had made such a scene in the Central Jamaican delegation which caused the delegation to revote by secret ballot, had up to six weeks before the Union session been strongly advocating that the union president not be reelected. He had accused him of consulting the obeah men (spiritualistic mediums) in Kingston, and he also accused him of being immoral. However, no evidence was ever presented to my knowledge which would suggest the validity of these accusations. Suddenly, however, six weeks before the constituency meeting there was a dramatic change, and this pastor began to urge church members to support the union president. It was only after the elections that it was revealed that the union president had told this pastor, who was the Central Jamaica Conference Stewardship Director, that if he were reelected this pastor would be elevated to the stewardship secretary of the Union.

Interestingly enough, neither the Cayman Island Mission Treasurer nor the pastor delegate from the Central Jamaica Conference ultimately were given their promised positions. However, it greatly disappointed me to think that men and women would sell their souls for "a mess of pottage." Better to be a "doorkeeper in the house of my God" (Psalm 84:10) than to compromise one's soul and jeopardize eternal life.

As the reports were being rendered to the rest of the delegates while the selection committee was choosing the nominating committee, it seemed that hardly a delegate was concentrating on the affairs of the union. Their only thought was, "What is happening in the selection committee room?" However within a couple of seconds of the door opening and the members of the selection committee walking out into the church sanctuary, it was clear to everyone that a committee had been voted that was in favor or reelecting the union president. As they entered the church sanctuary, the expressions upon the faces told it all. Those who were known to be supporters of the union president's reelection were beaming with joy; the rest were entering with glum expressions on their faces. At that time the union president and the union treasurer were seated on the platform. They looked to their left, and they too burst out in beaming smiles. No one had to hear the result. It was plain from the faces.

When the college's delegate, Elder Davis, came out, I could see how distressed he was. I nudged him and said, "Well, Elder, what happened?" He told me, and this was confirmed by others, that when the delegate from the college was to be chosen to the nominating committee, Elder Davis jumped to his feet. No one else jumped, but one of the pro-union president's supporters, while remaining seated, called out the name of the only delegate from the college who was likely to support the union president. That was the dean of students. Elder Davis was distraught that he would be seen as letting the college down. But, of course, it had not been his fault. When there was a great protest that Elder Davis was the first on his feet, it was alleged that the division president said, "Well, it has been getting a little disorganized. We will have to accept this nomination."

At that point many of the delegates left the session. They knew it was all over. It had been dishonest, and they would take no further part in the session. However, I decided it was my responsibility to stay and vote against the reelection of the president. It was made more difficult when the division president asked those in favor of the reelection of the union president to please stand. This happened with the president of the Union sitting on the platform, and he could see those who stood. I was so disappointed to see many of the men standing whom I knew had "convictions" in the other direction. But once the nominating committee made its decision they were too weak to stand upon their "conviction." Others did not stand but when they asked for a show of "those opposed," only nine of us stood. I knew that that would be the end of my ministry in Jamaica. No one who directly opposed would be allowed to continue in his position of authority for long. Thus my wife and I began to make plans to leave. It did not eventuate until several months later.

I regretted my actions after the election. I approached the division president and in great anger told him I had never seen such disgraceful behavior by a division president. While it was true that I needed to speak with him, I should have shown the courtesy and Christlikeness that Christians should always portray. Paul says:

> Rebuke not an elder, but intreat him as a father; and the younger men as brethren. 1 Timothy 5:1

God had further work for me to do, and He led me to Columbia Union College as chairman of the Psychology Department. Six months later I was chosen academic dean of the college, and two months after that president of the college. I had no idea that someone who had had so little experience in American style education as I had had would have such a meteoric rise to the presidency of an American college. But I look back and know that God was preparing me for an even greater work ahead.

By God's grace I was able to make things right with the division president two years later. We were both delegates to the Annual Council held in 1974 at the Loma Linda University Church. On the final evening Elder Robert Pierson, then General Conference president, made an urgent appeal to all of us that should we have anything against any other brother there, we were to make it right. I resisted. Always in my thought was the belief that it was the division president who had done wrong, not me. But then the Lord placed in my mind:

> Therefore if thou bring thy gift to the altar, and there rememberest that thy brother hath ought against thee; leave there thy gift before the altar, and go thy way; first be reconciled to thy brother, and then come and offer thy gift. Matthew 5:23–24

Whether I was right or wrong in the issue, I had to make wrongs right. My anger was a sin. Also, I had not followed the counsel of the Lord which says the younger is to entreat the elder. This I had not done.

I returned to my motel room after Elder Pierson's appeal but could not sleep. For at least two hours I tossed and turned until I told the Lord that first thing in the morning I would contact the division president. That I did from the airport before I left, and I had peace again. Indeed, since then we have had good fellowship together. By the way, about two years before the death of the union president, who was then retired in Florida and not in the best of health, I took my family to visit him, and we had a very blessed time together. It was a great lesson to me that not only must we be *right,* but we have to be very *Christlike* in how we respond in the most displeasing situations. [Note: As this book goes to press, I have received word that the division president has recently passed to his rest.]

Leaving Jamaica was not easy, for Cheryl and I left many friends behind, some of whom we never saw again. However, we hope to join them in the heavenly home. God has greatly blessed our ministry since leaving Jamaica, but we will never forget the blessings we received in our ministry there.

Index

Scripture References
Exodus 32:6 94
Job 1:21 139
Psalm 34:7 50
Psalm 84:10 152
Psalm 91:7 115
Psalm 127:4–5 73
Matthew 5:23–24 154
Matthew 16:26 66
Mark 8:36–37 22
John 18:36 103
Romans 7:24 54
Romans 8:2 58
Romans 8:3 62
1 Timothy 5:1 153
2 Timothy 4:1–5 35
Hebrews 2:14-18 63
Hebrews 4:15 63
Revelation 3:17 54

Spirit of Prophecy References
Counsels on Diet and Foods,
    pp. 380–381 41
Counsels to Parents, Teachers, and Students,
    pp. 343–344 97
    p. 350 ....96, 117
Education, pp. 210–211 97
Fundamentals of Christian Education,
    p. 293 82
    p. 478 102
Review and Herald, December 15, 1896 ..63
Selected Messages, book 3, p. 129 63
Signs of the Times, June 18, 1902 89
Spiritual Gifts, vol. 4a, p. 115 63
Testimonies for the Church,
    vol. 2, p. 352 42
    vol. 9, pp. 153-154 42

Institutions
Andrews Memorial Church 22
Andrews Memorial Hospital 7, 31, 91
Atlantic Union College 36
Avondale College 5
Black Muslim Organization 113
Caribbean Union College 36
Gordon House 19, 21
Jamaican Labor Party 98
Loma Linda University Church 10
Pacific Union College 70
People's National Party 98
Port Maria Church 115
Port Maria High School 112
Queen's College 85
Robin's Bay Church 108
Southern Missionary College 20
United Student Movement 17, 125
West Indies College Academy 48

Personalities
Anderson, Dr. Clifford 7
Anderson, Pastor O.K. 7
Andrews, Dr. 148
Archibold, Elder Bender 34
Barnes, Aston 27
Barnes, Linnie 28
Bennett, Harold 85
Brodie, Del 31
Brodie, Glad 31
Brooks, Elder Charles D. 132
Brown, Dr. Walter 13
Carey, Jean 79
Cato, Vernon 114
Cheeseman, Mr. And Mrs. 16
Chisholm, Lourine 30
Christopher, Carlton 104, 105, 107

155

Crabbe, Brian 12
Davis, Elder Aston 27, 149, 152
Davis, Zenobia 28
Doc, Baby 57
Doc, Papa 56
Douce, Dr. Herman 27, 88, 90, 124
Dower, Elder Reggie 132
Forrester, Faith 85
Frame, Pastor Robert 7
Franz, Clyde 135
Gallimore, Dr. Neville 19, 70, 99
Green, Mr. 46
Hirsch, Dr. Charles 7, 34
Howell, Mae 31
Hughes, Cassius Boone 80
Jones, Colville 87
Larson, Dr. Ralph 61
Lashley, Elder 36
Lashley, Sylvan 36
Long, Mr. 129
Lyle, Pastor Albert 130
Mahabee family 137
Maise, Josh 118
Manley, Michael 20
Manley, Norman Washington 20
McLaren, Dr. Gilbert 7
Medina, Dr. 68
Murdoch, Dr. William 123
Nembhard, Elder Hilbert 24, 28, 87,
....105, 119, 140
Nembhard, Elder Melvin 133
Nembhard, Millicent 28
Nembhard, Sister 53
Neufeld, Dr. 67, 69
Parchment, Edna 30
Pierson, Elder Robert 132, 153
Pratt, Dr. Lloyd 68
Rippon, Dr. Barton 12
Rugless, Admah 28
Rugless, Elder Oswald 24, 28, 88, 149
Rugless, Sister 90
Sams, Pastor 34
Scavella, Pastor Neville 118, 120
Seaga, Edward 19, 21
Shearer, Hugh 98

Standish, Nigel 29
Standish, Russell 32, 61
Steed, Elder Ernest 12
Taylor, Pastor Wesley 60, 61
Toussant, Brother 56
Vaz, Elder Kenneth 13, 29
Vivienne 23, 89
Walters, Elder H.S. 5, 7, 13, 14, 17, 33, 98
Walters, Lucille 19, 29, 90, 119
Walters, Vickie 79
White, Daisy 30
White, Joan 88
Williams, Elder Roy 81, 82
Wilson, Valerie 108
Wong, Professor 148

Topics Not Mentioned in Titles
Ackee 39
Agricultural show 83
Bus journey across the United States 10
Crime rate in Jamaica 44
Death in the Hospital 67
Death Threats 44
Devil Possession 23, 85
Devil possession 58, 92
Explosion of hot water heater 37
Flesh food 39
Hawaii, stopover in 9
Ingathering 75
Integrity, Men of 27
Jamaica
    Call to 5
    First arrival in 13
    Journey from Australia to 8
Los Angeles, first arrival at 10
National politics 70, 98, 99, 102
Ordination to the Gospel Ministry 32
Parliament, first visit to Jamaican 19
Rebel Leader in Anguilla 64
Sports 93, 117
Stink peas 53
Voodoo 56
Water shortages 51

Hartland Publications Book List

These books may be ordered from Hartland Publications (see the last page of this book for complete contact information). Many of these books are also available from Highwood Books in Australia: 03–59637011

Books by Colin Standish and Russell Standish
(Unless otherwise noted as by one or the other)

The 144,000, the Great Multitude, and the Return of Jesus

Fascinating as it has been to many Christians, few have solved the mystery of the 144,000 and the great multitude of the book of Revelation. Yet the pioneers of the Seventh-day Adventist Church focused much attention upon them. Like a sudden and unexpected flash of blinding lightning the 144,000 are introduced in Revelation 7 and again in Revelation 14, never again to be mentioned. The Old Testament is silent on the topic; Christ said nothing about it; neither did the writers of the gospels or the apostolic epistles. Yet the authors solve most of the divisive interpretations from the Bible itself and show how important is the understanding of these groups to all Christians.

Adventism Imperiled—Education in Crisis (230 pages)

In this newly revised edition of the most penetrating books written on Adventist education, the Standish brothers go directly to the word of God for the principles by which children that are called to be the sons and daughters of the King of the universe are to be educated. Every Seventh-day Adventist interested in our children and youth should read this book. Both authors are trained educators, having spent decades in education from the elementary to university level.

Adventism Proclaimed (202 pages)

In answer to "When shall these things be and what shall be the sign of thy coming, and the end of the world?" (Matthew 24:3), Jesus related many signs. One of those signs (verse 14) has captivated the authors—"This gospel of the kingdom shall be preached in all the world for a witness unto all nations: and then shall the end come." In the context of the 3 Angels Messages, this is what shall go forth with the power of the loud cry of Revelation 18:1–5. "To every nation, and kindred, and tongue and people." (Revelation 14:6) You will feel compelled to share with others, and be motivated to prepare urgently for the coming of the Lord.

Adventism Vindicated (141 pages)

The late 1970s was a time when the new theology was rapidly engulfing a confused and uncertain Seventh-day Adventist Church as a reaction to legalistic principles. Tragically, many who found the impotency of legalism were deceived into accepting a theology that claims that there are no divine conditions of salvation–a belief that victorious Christian living is not possible and has no mandate in salvation. This book answers the writings of Jack Sequeira as they relate to the precious message of "Christ our Righteousness" given at the 1888 General Conference in Minneapolis.

The Antichrist Is Here (185 pages)

A newly updated, second edition! Colin and Russell Standish have extensively researched the historical identification of the antichrist of past generations and are convinced the antichrist is present on earth now. They have taken those events which have transpired in the last decade and measured them in the light of biblical prophecy. You will read undeniable evidence in support of their findings. A "must-read" for those who are interested in biblical prophecy and its outworking in contemporary history.

The Big Bang Exploded (218 pages)

For decades the "big bang" hypothesis has held sway as the dominant explanation of the origin of the universe. It has proven to be a remarkably enduring hypothesis, yet the determined efforts of scientists from many disciplines have failed to provide confirmation of this hypothesis.

The authors assert that the "big bang theory" and Darwin's proposal of natural selection are "spent, decayed and archaic theories." The Standish brothers seriously address some of the most startling challenges to this theory of origins. They present evidence which they assert supports, far more closely, the fiat creation concept than the evolutionary model. This is another of the increasing challenges which evolutionary scientists must address if their credibility is not to be seriously undermined.

Deceptions of the New Theology (290 pages)

The term "new theology" was made prominent in the 1970s with the presentation by a number of popular preachers in the Seventh-day Adventist Church who taught what appeared to many to be a beautiful, new, Christ-centered emphasis. However, the ultimate results have been seen in untold thousands leaving the Seventh-day Adventist church, including many ministers and denominational workers. The answer to the eternal destructiveness of this movement is to uphold the authentic Christ.

Education for Excellence (174 pages)

This book goes directly to the word of God for educational principles for the sons and daughters of the King of the Universe. In the ministry of the apostle Paul, the culture, philosophy and education of paganism was confronted by the principles of God-given education. Though the world of his day was under the political rulership of Rome, Greece still controlled the mind, and therefore the educational processes of the Mediterranean. As Paul's ministry led him to city after city under the influence of Greek education and philosophy, it was necessary for him to define clearly the differences between pagan and Christian education. Most cultures today face the continued influence of paganistic education. Many who claim to support Christian education nevertheless are not fully aware of the complete contrasts between the two. Christianity wholly defines the curriculum, the teacher selection, the teaching methodology, the extracurricular activities, etc. Its goals, purposes and objectives are entirely different from secular education.

Embattled Church (143 pages)

The SDA church faces a crisis! Confusion and division are rampant. Assurance of truth has surrendered to uncertainty. Surety of faith has given way to an enfeebling pluralism. Uniqueness has been overcome by ecumenicalism. The sense of urgency has been replaced by carnal security. The spiritual church has become a social club. Unwavering loyalty is now branded as bigotry. Faithfulness to Christ is judged legalism. The defenders of truth are spurned as schismatics. The state of the church has led untold thousands to reevaluate their relationship to it. This book addresses this issue of separation.

The Entertainment Syndrome (116 pages)

This book explores how the large increase in entertainment impacts the physical, emotional, social, intellectual and spiritual life of the human race, and the devastating effect of its use in our churches.

The European Union, the American Union, the Papacy, and Globalism

The book of Revelation reveals a powerful global movement just prior to the return of Christ—a moment which is deeply riveted in both politics and religion. They provide evidence that the Papacy is the religious backbone of this movement as it postures to become the superpower upon the planet. They explain the reason why this globalism will lead to the greatest tyranny this planet has ever witnessed and how every major unit of society will continue to support this globalism. The authors present evidence from biblical prophecy that this global thrust will not completely be achieved and how the world will be liberated from ruthless globalists.

The Evangelical Dilemma (222 pages)

There has never been a more urgent time for an honest review of the past, present and future of Evangelical Protestantism. The authors present an examination of the major doctrinal errors of Evangelical Protestants.

The Everlasting Gospel (368 pages)

This book is written for all sincere Christians of all faiths. The authors have been puzzled why so many Christians strongly believe "the gospel" and yet ignore the central theme of the gospel. The authors have preached this gospel on every inhabited continent of the world and now they present it in a fascinating, simply explained presentation in this book for all to understand and share with others.

The Gathering Storm and The Storm Burst (421 pages)

The Gathering Storm **(Part 1)**—The Seventh-day Adventist Church experienced a tragic and dramatic redirection of its doctrines and practices beginning in the mid-1950s. While many were aware of this, few knew the almost unbelievable story behind this great apostasy. In this section, formerly entitled *Adventism Challenged A*, the authors have traced the only authentic, comprehensive development of this tragic area in God's remnant Church. Remarkably, God placed them in situations that allowed them to be eyewitnesses to the unfolding events. This book will challenge every reader who is loyal to Christ to rise up on behalf of God, His Word and His Truth.

The Storm Burst **(Part 2)**—The ease with which previous heresies successfully invaded the Seventh-day Adventist Church had been of great shock to all faithful members. Though we have been warned constantly that it would happen, its reality has come as a whirlwind into our midst. *Adventism Challenged B* continues to detail how the new theology was imported from Australia to the United States and other parts of the world. The authors document the earnest efforts of many current leaders, former leaders, and laity, to stay the plague of unfaithfulness to the truth and mission of the SDA Church.

The General Conference Confronts Apostasy (640 pages)

While a number of excellent histories of the Seventh-day Adventist church have been written, *The General Conference Confronts Apostasy* is unique. No other historical volume has documented in detail the manner in which church leaders have dealt with apostasy in our midst from its earliest times. Commencing with fanatical worship services, moving to the Messenger and the Marian offshoots, then to the entry of what is now commonly known as the "new theology" with the defection of Pastor Dudley Canright, this book takes up the earth-shattering 1888 General Conference session, the promotion of pantheism, the "holy flesh" movement of Indiana in 1900, hierarchical church governance, the issue of self-supporting work, the military issue of World War I, and the trend-setting 1919 Bible conference. *The General Conference Confronts Apostasy* examines each one in detail, presenting the impact upon God's Church in the twenty-first century.

Georgia Sits On Grandpa's Knee (R. Standish) (86 pages)
World-traveler Russell Standish delights in visiting with his little grand-daughter, Georgia. She loves to sit on her grandpa's knee and hear stories of "the old times" when her daddy was a little boy in Australia, Malaysia, Thailand, England, and Singapore. And it is Dr. Standish's delight to also share these tales of a family era now past—the joys of life together in exotic lands. Georgia thinks that other children will enjoy her grandpa's stories. Grandpa hopes so, too!

God's Other Arm (106 pages)
Self-supporting ministries, independent ministries, supporting ministries—sometimes there seems to be utter confusion in the Seventh-day Adventist church today about their roles. Some church members believe that the denominational work is so paralyzed by apostasy, worldliness, and corruption that lay ministries are the only hope for finishing the gospel commission. Others militantly oppose lay ministries, labeling them schismatics, divisive, separationists, cultists, and offshoots.

God's Solution for Depression, Guilt and Mental Illness (229 pages)
This powerful book argues with great persuasiveness that God is interested in every aspect of His created beings and that the perfect answers to man's needs are to be found in the Word of God.

Grandpa, You're Back! (R. Standish) (128 pages)
Pastor Russell Standish again delights and fascinates his granddaughter, Georgia, with stories of his many travels to countries ranging from South America to such far-flung places as Singapore, Africa, and beyond. These stories should pleasantly awaken the imagination of young readers.

The Greatest of All the Prophets (411 pages)
In 2004, under the guise of protecting the Spirit of Prophecy, the South Pacific Division launched an eight-pronged attack against the Testimonies of God. This book thoroughly documents the attack and the parallel defaming of Scripture. The claimed errors of Scripture and the Spirit of Prophecy are examined in detail and refuted. The book sets forth the inerrant, infallible character of God's inspired messages. It establishes our faith, essential for those who love and trust God and truly desire salvation. It sets forth and exposes the fearful sophistries which are deceiving God's people today. This is a book for every church leader, theologian, pastor, elder and member. It is a book for its time.

Gwanpa and Nanny's Home (R. Standish and Ella Rankin) (128 pages)

"I am Ella Marie Rankin. I want to tell you about Gwanpa's and Nanny's home. But I have a problem! You see, I'm only three and I haven't yet learned to write. So, my Gwanpa is writing my story for me." So begins a book that Russell Standish wrote for his granddaughter.

Half a Century of Apostasy (480 pages)

This book covers the grim harvest of the "new theology" during the years of 1956 to 2006. It is the Mount Carmel in God's Seventh-day Adventist Church today. The words of the prophet Elijah, destined to be translated, echo in our ears once more: "How long halt ye between two opinions? if the LORD be God, follow him: but if Baal, then follow him" (1 Kings 18:21). Never in any book, outside Scripture and the Spirit of Prophecy, has a volume been written which has set forth so clearly the manifest departure from God's pure truth by His Church. Each brief chapter is an urgent call for reform in the power of the Holy Spirit. It is the authors' prayer that this book will open the eyes of the spiritually blind and help to prepare the hearts of sincere believers as each prepares for translation.

Handbook for Lay and Self-Supporting Workers (255 pages)

This handbook provides essential information, guidance, and practical information to enhance the ministry of both new and experienced lay workers, written by men who have founded successful lay ministries. Their wealth of information will provide a strong platform for avoiding numerous pitfalls and gaining new insights into a Spirit-filled, soul-saving ministry.

Holy Relics or Revelation (300 pages)

Biblical archaeologists have gathered data with painstaking effort, and their work proves the accuracy of the Bible. Yet, mostly within a single decade, Ron Wyatt had sought out and claimed the most amazing biblical sites and relics. In this book, the Standish Brothers examine the Wyatt claims in-depth. Their findings serve as a benchmark upon which Ron Wyatt's "discoveries" can be more carefully evaluated.

Keepers of the Faith (240 pages)

As every wind of doctrine is marshaled against the church, more determined efforts are required to alert and warn of the dangers and errors that are now endemic in most congregations. In this book, the authors have attempted to identify and explain clearly the nature of many of these errors, and to document the clear truth as revealed by Inspiration. The book is especially directed to gospel ministers and lay leaders in the church. Previous editions of the book have found wide circulation among rank-and-file laity who discovered it to be one of the clearest presentations of biblical principles of truth and righteousness.

Liberty in the Balance (263 pages)

The bloodstained pathway to religious and civil liberty faces its greatest test in 200 years. The United States "Bill of Rights" lifted the concept of liberty far beyond the realm of toleration to an inalienable right for all citizens. Yet, for a century and a half, some students of the prophecies of John the Revelator have foretold a time just prior to the return of Christ when these most cherished freedoms will be wrenched from the citizens of the United States, and the U.S. would enforce its coercive edicts upon the rest of the world. This book traces the courageous battle for freedom, a battle stained with the lives of many martyrs.

The Lord's Day (310 pages)

In his famous encyclical *Dies Domini*, Pope John Paul II commenced with these words, "The Lord's Day—as Sunday was called from apostolic times. . . ." To many Protestants, this was an unexpected and much-approved declaration from the Roman Catholic supreme pontiff. The issue of the apostolic origin of Sunday-worship has often been a contentious one between Roman Catholics and Protestants. This book presents an in-depth examination of the Sabbath in the Scriptures.

Missionary To Jamaica (176 pages)

Nothing compares with foreign missionary service in a land far away from home and in a country whose culture is widely different from your own. Through this book you will "live" some of the joys, blessings, and miracles along with the frustrations, death threats, tragic experiences, and complex issues Colin and Cheryl Standish had to face. They will introduce you to a fascinating nation, culture, and vibrant people—a people they learned to love dearly and in so many ways to respect. This book is for those of all ages who love missionary stories.

Modern Bible Translations Unmasked (228 pages); Supplement (30 pages)

This fascinating book challenges the reader to consider two very serious problems with modern translations: first, the use of corrupted Greek manuscripts, and second, translational bias. The authors are deeply concerned about the paraphrases and some of the efforts to translate the Bible into colloquial language, but they are also deeply concerned about the more respected translations that are gaining great acceptance in today's society. You will learn how these modern translations are reinforcing false teachings and erroneous gospel presentations. The supplement contains Spirit of Prophecy quotations and other materials for Seventh-day Adventists on this important topic.

The Mystery of Death (128 pages)
There are those today who believe that the soul is immortal and externally preexisted the body. Pagan or Christian, the opinions vary widely. In this book, the history of these concepts is reviewed and the words of Scripture are investigated for a definitive and unchallengeable answer.

Organizational Structure and Apostasy (164 pages)
This new reprint of *The Temple Cleansed* specifically details the way the organizational structure of the SDA Church is being molded after the deadly hierarchal pattern of the world. Few understand the simple organizational pattern that God provided for His church at all denominational and local levels—therefore, few raise the alarm. The eyes of the discerning reader should be opened to the type of organization God will have in place when he cleanses His church. The human machinery will be swept aside.

Perfection (45 pages)
The Bible teaches perfection of character, not perfection of flesh or nature. This book helps the leader to fully understand the Bible's teaching of perfection of character in all of its aspects.

Perils of Ecumenism (416 pages)
The march of ecumenism seems unstoppable. From its humble roots after the first World War, with the formation of the Faith and Order Council at Edinburgh University, Scotland, and the Works and Labor Council at Oxford University, England, to the formation of the World Council of Churches in 1948 in Amsterdam, it has gained breathtaking momentum. The authors see the ecumenical movement as very clearly identified in Holy Scriptures as the movement devised by the arch-deceiver to beguile the inhabitants of the world.

Perils of Time Setting (82 pages)
This book demonstrates the failure of every time setting prediction ever made since 1844. It gives conclusive evidence that such time setting has its foundations in the Jesuit scheme to derail the Protestant Reformation and to refocus Protestants from their unwavering identification of the Papacy as the historical Antichrist of prophecy. It is an invaluable guide as to how to avoid being trapped by tantalizing but false principles of biblical interpretation.

The Pope's Letter and Sunday Laws (116 pages)
The authors examine the biblical foundations upon which the pope seeks to buttress his apostolic letter, *Dies Domini*. But even the undoubted skill of the pope and his

scholarly advisors cannot mask the fallacies of the pope's conclusions. The authors show emphatically that the pope's assertions are in deep contradiction to the record of the Holy Bible and that of history.

Postmodernism and the Decline of Christianity

Like stealth in the night, postmodernism has not only invaded the world but the church. It is a concept in which there are no universal laws, no ultimates, no immutables. It is a belief which developed out of the modernist world, though it has gone far beyond modernism. It is based upon the feelings of each individual. Truth is nothing more than the whims of each individual. Few Christians have understood the postmodernist agenda, let alone the profound influence it has exerted upon the Christian church. This book exposes how far this influence has invaded the portals of the Christian establishments and how it is destroying the very fabric of society.

The Rapture and the Antichrist (288 pages)

This book sets forth the plainest truths of Scripture directing Protestantism back to its biblical roots. It will challenge the thinking of all Christians, erase the fictions of the *Left Behind* Series, and plant the reader's spiritual feet firmly on the platform of Scripture.

The Rapture, the End Times and the Millennium (378 pages)

This book will open the minds of the readers to a clear understanding of areas of the end-time which have led to much perplexity among lay-people and theologians alike. It is also guaranteed to dispel many of the perplexities presently confronting those who are searching for a clear biblical exposition of the last cataclysmic days in which we now live.

Reflections on Eight General Conference Sessions (112 pages)

A thirty-five year span can be a significant period in the history of any church, especially in the bewildering world in which we now live. How has God's chosen, remnant church fared during this period of earth's history? Most churches during the last thirty-five years in Christendom have taken very sharp turns toward ecumenism, Pentecostalism, Roman Catholicism, and worldly practices. How has our beloved church fared? This book examines the answer to this question through the evaluations of eight consecutive General Conference Sessions. Few delegates or visitors have attended eight consecutive General Conference sessions but one of the authors has. This review of the actions taken, messages presented, and the activities undertaken will be of deep interest to church members and church leaders alike.

The Road to Rome (217 pages)
Sister White wrote, "The Omega of Apostasy will be of a most startling nature." (*Selected Messages*, Vol. 1, pg. 197) She also stated—"The church has turned back from following Christ, her Leader, and is steadily retreating toward Egypt." (*Testimonies*, Vol. 1, pg. 217) The time is overdue for us to evaluate how far we have traveled down the Road To Rome! With deep sensitivity and a passionate love for their church, the authors have uncovered what many will recognize as an orchestrated plan to systematically implement the catholicizing of the Seventh-day Adventist Church.

The Sacrificial Priest (272 pages)
To all Christians the centrality of the sacrifice of Christ on Calvary has been the focus of their salvation hopes. However, relatively few Christians have understood the equally important ministry of Christ in the heavenly sanctuary. The authors provide a fascinating biblical explanation and irrefutable evidence of this little-studied high priestly ministry of Christ in the heavenly sanctuary.

The Second Coming (80 pages)
The Apostle Paul refers to the second coming of Jesus as the blessed hope. (Titus 2:12) Yet, soon after the death of all the apostles, doubts and debates robbed the people of this assurance and brought in the pagan notion of immediate life after death. In this new updated work, Colin and Russell Standish present a "wake-up call" for every complacent Christian.

The Sepulchres Are Whited (301 pages)
We are at the end of probationary time. If God's church is to receive the full outpouring of the latter rain, there must be a return to truth and righteousness. This alone will provide the unity that God can honor with His Spirit. This book is written to stimulate such a reformation in our ranks.

Spiritism in the SDA Church (133 pages)
The authors believe that every deviation from truth has its root in spiritism. They take a broad concept of spiritism to include idolatry, paganism, humanism, New Age philosophy, Catholicism and Satanism, and explore some surprisingly "respectable" forms of spiritism that are designed especially for the more wary Christian. This book reveals the frightening inroads of spiritualistic theory and practice that has become deeply embedded within much of contemporary Seventh-day Adventism.

Tithes and Offerings—Trampling The Conscience (112 pages)
With unreasonable fervor and scant knowledge, many have sought to condemn God's ordained self-supporting ministries that accept tithe for their soul saving gospel

work. This has led the tithe issue to become a religious liberty issue in God's Church. This book is a remarkable contribution to our understanding of this topic. The authors have researched the tithe issue to a depth never before attempted, and have again done what they do best–bring an issue back to the objective evidence of God's sacred Word and the Spirit of Prophecy.

Twenty-eight Fundamentals: Apostasy Proclaimed in Silence (234 pages)

Throughout the history of God's church on earth the insinuation of apostasy has been achieved, not so much in open pronouncements, but by guile and stealth. Silence has been the major weapon upon which error has comfortably rested. By subtlety it has found a foothold in God's church. Through this stratagem, the initial tolerance of both precious truth and damnable error, a channel has been opened so that sacred principles of faith and the destructive errors of Satan have been permitted, for a season, to lie together as bedfellows. This ploy has served the cause of Satan all too well. It has, in turn, led ultimately to the spurning of truth.

Two Beasts, Three Deadly Wounds and Fifteen Popes (234 pages)

Revelation 13 presents two incomprehensible beasts—one of which received a deadly wound in one of its heads. Prophecy stated that this mortal injury would be healed, and that the power represented by the beast would be admired worldwide. The authors give a detailed history of the fifteen popes who have sat upon the papal throne since the infliction of the deadly wound. The reader will find compelling evidence that the deadly wound is now so well-healed that there remains virtually no trace of the scar. For students of Scripture, this book will enlighten and bring an understanding of biblical prophecy and perhaps a new appreciation of the conclusive accuracy of Bible prophecy. The authors present this book as for all minds, a challenge to all hearts, and a timely wake-up call for humanity.

Uncle Russell and Daddy Stories (208 pages)

When Colin's children, Nigel and Alexandra, were growing up, he frequently told them stories and lessons gleaned from events in the life of Colin and his twin brother Russell during the time they were boys and youth growing up in Australia. These stories included the surprise birth of Colin and Russell, some of the challenges of the depression years, up to their college graduation. Although the stories are not always flattering to two boys born into a very poor but deeply dedicated family, they provide unique, first-hand insights into the happenings and events which were to lay the foundation for a lifetime of service for the Savior.

The Vision and God's Providences (C. Standish): Unabridged (240 pages); Abridged (176 pages)

The story of the development of Hartland Institute must be attributed to God alone. Yet, many men and women have had the privilege of being His humble instruments to contribute to Hartland's establishment. This book recalls divine leadings, human weakness, misunderstandings, and strong differences of opinion, and we cannot but wonder what God might have accomplished, had we listened perfectly to His voice.

Why Members Leave the Seventh-day Adventist Church (256 pages)

The authors have developed a great concern for the terrible carnage of members in the Seventh-day Adventist Church. When they were children in Australia there was great concern because 30 percent of children born into the Seventh-day Adventist homes were choosing to walk away from the Church. However, several years ago they were staggered to learn that now 81 percent of the Church's youth were abandoning the Seventh-day Adventist Church in Australia and New Zealand. They also learned that an alarming number of members who had been added through evangelistic outreach soon thereafter walk away from the church. In this book the authors share the Divine solutions to the many different ways that Satan has found to achieve this deplorable situation.

Winds of Doctrine (174 pages)

Satan has not confined his attacks to denominational workers and leaders, but has also attacked those in the self-supporting work. The tragedy is that some have accepted the nefarious subtleties of Satan and have led many that are not stabilized in the faith away from truth and righteousness. This book is essential reading for all earnest Seventh-day Adventists. It takes up the issues central to the apostasy—the name of God, the Godhead, the Person of the Holy Spirit, the eternal existence of Christ, the Wednesday crucifixion, the correct Sabbath hours, and God's destructive judgment.

Youth, Are You Preparing for Your Divorce? (168 pages)

A majority of youth, including Christian youth, are destined for divorce. Yes, you read this correctly! Unbeknown to them or to their parents, long before marriage or even courtship, the seeds of divorce have been sown to later produce their baneful consequences. Many youth who think they are preparing for marital bliss are preparing for divorce and, all too frequently, their parents are co-conspirators in this tragedy. The authors provide amazing simple principles to avert the likelihood of future divorce.

Youth Do You Dare! (C. Standish) (88 pages)

If you are a young person looking for workable answers to the many issues that confront you today, this book is for you. It presents a call to young people to follow truth and righteousness, and to live morally upright lives.

Other Books from Hartland Publications

Behold the Lamb—David Kang (107 pages)

God's plan of redemption for this world and the preservation of the universe is revealed in the sanctuary which God constructed through Moses. This book explains the sanctuary service in the light of the Christian's personal experience. Why this book? Because Jesus is coming soon!

China Letters—David Lin (428 pages)

Applies the hammer of truth to the tensile of New Theology, exposing the nature of the base metal for what really is, not gold or silver, but rather tin and dross. These collected letters and articles appeared in various Adventist periodicals at a time when Ford's teachings were the center of attention in the SDA church.

Christ and Antichrist—Samuel J. Cassels (348 pages)

First published in 1846 by a well-known Presbyterian minister, who called this book "not sectarian, but a Christian and Protestant work." He hoped that the removal of obstacles might result in a more rapid spread of the Gospel. One of these obstacles he saw as "Antichristianity," a term he that he used to describe the Papal system.

Distinctive Vegetarian Cuisine—Sue M. Weir (329 pages)

100% vegan cooking, with no animal products—no meat, milk, eggs, cheese, or even honey. No irritating spices or condiments are used. Most of the ingredients can be found at your local market. There are additional nutritional information and helpful hints. Make your dinner table appealing to the appetite!

Food for Thought—Susan Jen (160 pages)

Where does the energy which food creates come from? What kinds of foods are the most conductive to robust health and well being in all dimensions of our life? What is a balanced diet? Written by a healthcare professional, this book examines the food we prepare for our table.

Group Think—Horace E. Walsh (96 pages)

Find out how a state of groupthink (or group dynamics) has often contributed to disaster in secular and spiritual matters, like the role of Hebrew groupthink in the rejection and ultimate crucifixion of the Son of God. Or, the Ecumenical Movement that seeks to unite the minds of dedicated men so much that their passion is to build one great super church following Rome.

Heroes of the Reformation—Hagstotz and Hagstotz (320 pages)

This volume brings together a comprehensive picture of the leaders of the Reformation who arose all over Europe. The authors of this volume have made a sincere endeavor to bring the men of Protestantism alive in the hearts of this generation.

His Mighty Love—Ralph Larson (159 pages)

Twenty-one evangelistic sermons! Every doctrine of the Bible is simply an answer to the question, "How does the love of God relate to this particular question or problem?" Every doctrine is further evidence that God is love! This book is divided into three sections with seven individual sermons each. Subjects range from "If God Is Almighty, Why Does He Permit Sin?" to "The Unpardonable Sin."

History of the Gunpowder Plot—Philip Sidney (303 pages)

Originally published on the 300th anniversary of the November 5, 1605, plot aimed at the destruction of the English Realm, is Philip Sydney's account of one of the most audacious conspiracies ever known to the ancient or modern. The failed plot became part of English popular culture.

The History of Protestantism—J. A. Wylie (2,136 pages)

This book pulls back the divine curtain and reveals God's hand in the affairs of His church during the Protestant Reformation. Your heart will be stirred by the lives of Protestant heroes, and your mind captivated by God's simple means to counteract the intrigues of its enemies. As God's church faces the last days, this compelling book will appeal and will be a blessing to adults as well as children.

History of the Reformation of the 16th Century—J. d'Aubigné (1,472 pages)

In history and in prophecy, the Word of God portrays the long continued conflict between truth and error. Today, we see an alarming lack of understanding in the Protestant Church concerning the cause and effect of the Reformation. This reprinted masterpiece pulls back the curtain of history and divine providence to reveal the true catalyst for the Reformation—God's Word and His Holy Spirit.

History of the Reformation in the Time of Calvin—d'Aubigné (1,971 pages)

The renovation of the individual, of the Church, and of the human race, is the theme. This renovation is, at the same time, an enfranchisement; and we might assign, as a motto to the Reformation accomplished by Calvin, as well as to apostolic Christianity itself, these words of Jesus Christ: The truth shall make you free. (John 8:32)

History of the Waldenses—J. A. Wylie (191 pages)

During the long centuries of papal supremacy, the Waldenses defied the crushing power of Rome and rejected its false doctrines and traditions. This stalwart people cherished and preserved the pure Word of God. It is fitting that this edition of their history should be reprinted to keep alive the spirit and knowledge of this ancient people.

Hus the Heretic—Poggius the Papist (78 pages)

One of the greatest of Reformers in history was John Hus. His pious life and witness during his trial and martyrdom convinced many of the priests and church leaders of his innocence and the justice of his cause. Poggius was the papal legate who delivered the summons to Hus to appear at the council of Constance, then participated member. This book consists of letters from Poggius to his friend Nikolai, and describes the trial and burning of Hus. So potent was John Hus' humble testimony, that even some of his ardent foes became his defenders.

The Law and the Sabbath—Allen Walker (149 pages)

A fierce controversy is swirling around the role the Ten Commandments should play in the church of the 21st Century. With a foreword by the late Elder Joe Crews, here is a book that dares to examine the Bible's own answers—with unfailing scriptural logic and a profound appreciation for the doctrine of righteousness by faith.

The Method of Grace—John Flavel (458 pages)

In this faithful reprint, John Flavel thoroughly outlines the work of God's Spirit in applying the redemptive work of Christ to the believer. Readers will find their faith challenged and enriched. In true Puritan tradition, a clearly defined theology is delivered with evangelistic fervor, by an author urgently concerned about the eternal destiny of the human soul.

The Reformation in Spain—Thomas M'Crie (272 pages)

The boldness with which Luther attacked the abuses and the authority of the Church in Rome in the 16th Century attracted attention throughout Christendom.

Luther's writings, along with the earlier ones of Erasmus, gained a foothold with a Spanish people hungry for the truth. Thomas M'Crie makes a case for a Spain free of the religious errors and corruptions that ultimately dried up the resources and poisoned the fountains of a great empire.

Romanism and the Reformation—H. Grattan Guinness (217 pages)

The Reformation of the 16th Century, which gave birth to Protestantism, was based on Scripture. It gave back to the world the Bible. Such Reformation work needs to be done again today. The duty of diffusing information on the true character and history of "Romanism and the Reformation" is one that presses on God's faithful people in these days.

Strange Fire—Barry Harker (206 pages)

The Olympic games are almost universally accepted as a great international festival of peace, sportsmanship, and friendly competition. Yet, the games are riddled with conflict, cheating, and objectionable competitiveness. Discover the disturbing truth about the modern Olympics and the role of Christianity in the rise of this neo-pagan religion.

The Third Angel's Message of Righteousness by Faith and Its Present Rejection—L. Scarborough (107 pages)

As Seventh-day Adventists, we tend to believe that our greatest danger of being deceived by error would come from without the church. Our concerns have been concentrated upon these varied forms of deceptions. We are far less prepared to stand against the deceptions that will come from within our own church.

Truth Triumphant—Benjamin George Wilkinson (440 pages)

The prominence given to the "Church in the Wilderness" in the Scriptures establishes without argument its existence and emphasizes its importance. The same challenges exist today with the Remnant Church in its final controversy against the powers of evil to show the holy, unchanging message of the Bible.

Who Are These Three Angels?—Jeff Wehr (126 pages)

The messages of three holy angels unfold for us events that are soon to take place. Their warning is not to be taken lightly. They tell of political and religious movements that signal the soon return of Jesus.

With Cloak and Dagger—H. H. Meyers (160 pages)
This is a startling revelation of a deliberate and successful effort by a small group of men to sabotage effectively the message and mission of God's remnant church. The basic fundamental principles that were endorsed by God's prophet to His remnant church as having "unquestionable authority," have since been systematically eroded and even changed!

The Word Was Made Flesh—Ralph Larson (365 pages)
One hundred years of Seventh-day Adventist Christology, from 1852 to 1952. This book is a comprehensive survey of the historical evidence of the human nature of Christ. "The nature of God, whose law had been transgressed, and the nature of Adam, the transgressor, meet in Jesus, the Son of God, and the Son of Man." Ellen White, *Manuscript 141*, 1901.

Youth Ministry in Crisis—Barry Harker (206 pages)
In this bracing book, Dr. Barry Harker examines the practices and passions that are transforming and debasing contemporary youth ministry—rock music, magic, clowning, comedy, drama, mime, puppetry, sports, extreme adventure activities, youth fashions and movies—and exposes the disturbing ideas that permit them to flourish in God's church. Dr. Harker also outlines steps that need to be taken if the enveloping crisis is to be resolved and youth ministry restored to a culture of defensible innovation. This book is a timely corrective to the ideas and practices that are defacing the image of God in His people.

True Education History Series from Hartland Publications

Livingstone—The Pathfinder—Basil Matthews (112 pages)

Like most boys and girls, David Livingstone wondered what he would become when he grew up. He had heard of a brave man who was a missionary doctor in China. He also learned that this Dr. Gulztoff had a Hero, Jesus, who had come to people as a healer and missionary. David learned all about this great Physician, and felt that the finest thing in the whole world for him was to follow in the same way and be a medical missionary. That was David's quest, which was his plan. Between these pages, you shall see how he made his good wish come true.

Missionary Annals—Memoir of Robert Moffat—M. L. Wilder (64 pages)

Robert Moffat first heard from his wise and pious mother's lips that there were heathen in the world and of the efforts of Christians sharing the knowledge of a Savior who could raise them out of their base degradation. An intense desire took possession of him to serve God in some marked manner but how that would be, he did not know. Through a series of providential circumstances and in God's good time, the London Society accepted him as one of their missionaries, and in 1816, he embarked on his first trip and got his first glimpse of heathen Africa. This book will inspire the young and old as you read the many trials, disappointments, triumphs, and wondrous miracles that God can accomplish when one is fully surrendered to Him.

The Waldenses—The Church in the Wilderness (72 pages)

The faithful Waldenses in their mountain retreats were married in a spiritual sense to God who promised, "I will betroth thee unto me in faithfulness and thou shalt know the Lord." (Hosea 2:20) No invention of Satan could destroy their union with God. Follow the history of these people as they are compared to the dedicated eagle parents.

Meet the Author

COLIN D. STANDISH was born in Newcastle, Australia, in 1933, a twin in a family of four children. He attended college and completed his Bachelor of Arts in psychology, with honors, at the University of Sydney. Colin completed his Master of Arts and Doctor of Philosophy, both in psychology, and then a second Master's in education.

Dr. Standish is currently president and pioneer of Hartland Institute in Rapidan, Virginia, which comprises a college, a wellness center, publishing house and a world mission division. Previously, he taught in the psychology department of the University of Sydney, and chaired the education department of Avondale College, Australia. He served as academic dean and president of West Indies College, Jamaica, and also as chairman of the psychology department, academic dean, and president of Columbia Union College, Maryland. He also served as dean of Weimar College, California.

He is the author of numerous books on Christian living. He enjoys music, nature, and spending time with his wife, Cheryl, and two children, Nigel and Alexandra. He has an enormous burden to help young people succeed mentally, spiritually and physically.

HARTLAND Publications was established in 1984 as a Bible-centered, self-supporting Protestant publishing house. We publish Bible-based books and produce media for Christians of all ages, to help them in the development of their personal characters, always giving glory to God in preparation for the soon return of our Lord and Savior, Christ Jesus. We are especially dedicated to reprinting significant books on Protestant history that might otherwise go out of circulation. Hartland Publications supports and promotes other Christian publishers and media producers who are consistent with biblical principles of truth and righteousness. We are seeking to arouse the spirit of true Protestantism, one that is based on the Bible and the Bible only, thus awakening the world to a sense of the value and privilege of the religious liberty that we currently enjoy.

Office hours (Eastern time):
Monday – Thursday: 9:00 a.m. to 5:00 p.m.
Friday: 9:00 a.m. to 12:00 noon

Payment must be in US dollars by check, money order, or most credit cards.

You may order via mail, telephone, fax, e-mail, or on the web site:

Hartland Publications
PO Box 1, Rapidan, VA 22733 USA

Order line: 1-800-774-3566 / Fax: 1-540-672-3568
E-mail: sales@hartlandpublications.org
Web site: www.hartlandpublications.com